Fortress MK.I Combat Log

Bomber Command High Altitude Bombing Operations

July – September 1941

Hugh Harkins

Fortress MK.I
Combat Log
Bomber Command High Altitude Bombing Operations
July – September 1941

© Hugh Harkins 2014

Published by Centurion Publishing
United Kingdom

ISBN 10: 1-903630-57-6
ISBN 13: 978-1-903630-57-0

This volume first published in 2014

The Publisher and Author would like to thank all organisations and services for their assistance and contributions in the preparation of this volume

FOR FLOYD

CONTENTS

INTRODUCTION

The purpose of this volume is to provide a comprehensive detailed study of the operational and combat operations of the RAF's Boeing Fortress MK.I (B-17C) long-range bombers which conducted a high altitude daylight bombing campaign over North West Europe and Norway during July, August and September 1941.

The volume covers Bomber Commands operational situation leading up to summer 1941 and details the early model Boeing B-17's including the B-17C, 20 of which were transferred to the RAF as Fortress MK.I bombers. The formation of No.90 Squadron RAF and the training and preparations for operations, including the transfer of USAAC ground and air crew which continued to operate with 90 Squadron throughout the bombing campaign. Although no USAAC personnel flew operational missions, the Corp suffered one of the Squadrons earliest casualties in a non-operational Fortress loss, and a gentleman from the American Sperry Bomb Sight Company flew one operational mission as bomb aimer.

The bombing campaign is described in detail with every operational sortie detailed, including targets, aircraft flown, weapons dropped, aircrew, and combats with German fighters; a number of Fortress I's being shot down.

A brief description of the genesis and development of the B-17 is laid down, but the volume is not intended to be a comprehensive monograph on that subject. The volume is copiously supported by a wealth of operational documents including Squadron Narratives and Squadron and Group Combat Reports, many of which are reproduced verbatim. Operational documents have been tied up against German records whenever possible.

THE FORTRESS MK.I AND BOMBER COMMAND

When Britain entered World War II on 3 September 1939 its bomber force consisted of a variety of light, medium and heavy bombers in the shape of the twin engine Bristol Blenheim and single engine Fairey Battle and twin engine Handley Page Hampden, Armstrong Whitworth Whitley and Vickers Wellington. Up to summer 1940, the bomber operations of both Germany and Britain had been restrained, with a few exceptions, being restricted to targets that could be easily justified as military in nature or support.

During the German invasion of France and the Low Countries in May and June 1940 the major focus of the Luftwaffe was on providing tactical support to its armies in the field, while the bomber forces were mainly focused on targeting infrastructure considered vital to the German offensive. It was during the intensive air battles of May 1940 that the RAF learned the painful lesson that its bombers were extremely vulnerable to enemy fighters and ground defenses when conducting large scale daylight operations. As losses mounted the RAF increasingly turned towards night bombing, although daylight bombing would continue on a reduced scale.

As the period known as the Battle of Britain was nearing its end going into winter 1940, the Germans too, at the end of a summer of heavy losses in aircraft and crews, turned more towards night bombing, although, like the British, they too would continue daylight bombing on a smaller scale than before.

In the United States the Boeing B-17 four-engine bomber was being developed as a high altitude long-range bomber for the USAAC (United States Army Air Corp). The RAF had no comparable high altitude bombers, nor any in development; the program of heavy bombers then being developed, the Avro Manchester, Short Stirling, Handley Page Halifax and Avro Lancaster, being developed mainly for the mass night bombing mission against area targets.

52273

The progenitor to what would become the B-17 Flying Fortress, the Boeing Model 299, unveiled by the Boeing Airplane Co. in 1935, was designed to compete for a USAAC requirement for a multi-engine bomber. USAF

The B-17B/C, while being vastly inferior to later aircraft like the Avro Lancaster, under development for the RAF, in areas such as load carrying capability, had a long range and could operate at higher altitudes. Such an aircraft, it was hoped, could give the RAF a viable heavy bomber capable of operating deep in enemy territory during daylight hours. While it was clear that the B-17 would not be immune to interception from German fighters which could reach the B-17's operating altitudes, the time it took for the intercepting fighters to reach those altitudes would vastly reduce the time available for interception, thus reducing losses in the attacking bomber force.

As with many aircraft programs there are many points in history which could be labelled as the start point for a particular project. For the purposes of this volume the 1934 US Army competition for a multi-engine bomber is as good a start as any. Boeing developed the Model 299, later designated XB-17, which conducted its maiden flight on 28 July 1935 and was destroyed in a crash on 30 October that year. The Model 299 was further developed into the Y1B-17A (B-17A), leading to the first production variant of the Flying Fortress, the B-17B, 39 of which were ordered by the USAAC, the first flying on 27 June 1939.

Top: Y1B-17 SN: 36-149 was the first of the service test aircraft, which were some 7 inches longer than the Model 299. Above: This Y1B-17, adorned with a disruptive camouflage scheme, belonged to the USAAC 20th Bomb Squadron, 2nd Bomb Group at Langley Field, Virginia. USAF

In 1940, the USAAC ordered a batch of 38 'improved' B-17B's, which were designated B-17C, the first of which flew on 21 July 1940. These aircraft were powered by four 1,200 hp. Wright R-1820-65 radial engines, however, the R.1820/73 engines equipped those examples sent to Britain for service with the RAF. The side waist gun blister positions of the B-17B were replaced by 'flat sliding gun panels; this having a number of advantages, including a more streamlined design and increased crew safety. Likewise, the ventral gun blister found in earlier models was replaced by a so called 'bathtub' turret, the Browning machine gun armament still proving to be susceptible to freezing at high altitudes.

The manufacturer's description of the B-17C states "The B-17C bombardment airplane is a midwing monoplane of all aluminum alloy stressed skin construction." "...each wing consists of an inboard panel, an outboard panel, a wing tip, a flap, and an aileron. A control tab is provided in the left aileron only. The four engine nacelles are incorporated in the two inboard panels. The empennage included the elevator panels, elevator control tabs, elevator trim tabs, horizontal stabilizer, vertical stabilizer, rudder, rudder control tab, and rudder trim tab. "... the fuselage is an all metal semi-monocoque aluminum alloy and steel structure." Emergency exits were located in the forward compartment through bulkhead door and the front entrance door; for the control cabin, through the top hatch of control cabin and through the bomb bay; for the radio compartment, through the bomb bay or main entrance; and for rear gun compartments, through the main entrance doorway.

The undercarriage "consists of a right and left assembly. Each assembly is of a single oleo cantilever type consisting of a strut and oleo assembly, torsion links, drag and retracting strut, wheel and brake. Retraction is normally accomplished by the electric motors operating simultaneously but emergency manual operation is provided for the right and left side and the tail wheel separately."

The British purchasing mission in the United States secured the transfer of 20 B-17C's to the RAF where they would be designated Fortress MK.I. The remaining B-17C's were later modified to B-17D standard. Although the British intention was to purchase the aircraft, some documentation refers to the aircraft being supplied as a gift from the United States.

The agreement for the transfer of the B-17C's to the RAF also included the transfer of a number of USAAC personnel, mainly to assist in training the initial RAF operators of the new bomber. However, some USAAC personnel remained in place during the Fortress I's initial operational career, a portent of things to come when formations of USAAF (United States Army Air Force), successor of the USAAC from June 1941, B-17's would operate on bombing missions over Europe, commencing in August 1942, following that countries entry into the war in December 1941.

Thirty nine B-17B's, the first of which conducted its maiden flight on 27 June 1939, were ordered for the USAAC; this being the first production variant for service use. USAF

As the first Fortress's were being absorbed into the RAF and prepared for operational service RAF Bomber Command was undergoing changes as its new heavy bombers were being introduced and the direction of its future offensive operations were being devised. "You will direct the main effort of the bomber force, until further instructions, towards dislocating the German transportation system, and to destroying the moral of the civil population as a whole, and of the industrial workers in particular". This was the directive issued to Air Marshal Sir Richard Peirse, Commander in Chief of Bomber Command on 9 July 1941; one day after the inaugural operation of No.90 Squadron with the Fortress I.

Much of Britain's bomber offensive had been geared towards attacks on naval targets and naval infrastructure in accordance with the wishes of the Admiralty, heavily embroiled in the Battle of the Atlantic. Since the dark days of the previous summer, when Britain faced a real threat of invasion, the bomber offensive had been conducted mainly by night; the light bombers of No.2 Group flying daylight raids on continental fringe targets, firstly to attack enemy targets as an anti-invasion measure and then as part of the overall air offensive over the continent, whereby large formations of British fighters would fly as cover to small formations of Bristol Blenheim IV bombers, which were in effect acting as bait to lure Luftwaffe fighters up to intercept whereby the German fighters could be engaged by the British fighters.

The B-17C (bottom) introduced many changes over the B-17B (top). The side waist gun blister positions of the B-17B were replaced by 'flat' sliding gun panels which had the advantage of being a more streamlined design with increased crew safety. The ventral gun blister found in earlier models was replaced by a so called 'bathtub' turret, however, the Browning machine gun armament continued to prove susceptible to freezing at high altitudes. USAF

In contrast with the previous summer when the RAF faced the bulk of the Luftwaffe bomber and fighter forces, the German presence in France and the Low Countries had been much reduced as Germany turned East, launching Operation Barbarossa, the Axis invasion of the Soviet Union, on 22 June 1941. From that point much of the RAF's role was aimed at attempting to tie down as much German forces in Western Europe as possible in order to assist the Soviets in their titanic struggle for survival as they faced the German onslaught.

Since the beginning of the war daylight bombing, particularly by unescorted bombers, had proven expensive in losses of aircraft and crews on both sides. No.2 Group was responsible for the bulk of Bomber Commands daylight operations, mainly Circus's, the first of which was flown on 14 January 1941, flying the standard light bomber then in service with the RAF, the Bristol Blenheim IV.

Going into 1941, the introduction of the new generation of British heavy bombers was underway. The first of these was the Short Stirling, the first of the RAF's four-engine heavy bombers. A half scale prototype had conducted its maiden flight in September 1938, followed by the full scale prototype, which flew in May 1939, and deliveries of production aircraft commenced to No.7 Squadron in August 1940, the first casualties being six aircraft destroyed on the production line during a Luftwaffe bombing raid.

The Stirling flew its first operational mission on the night of 10/11 February 1941 when No.7 Squadron bombed Rotterdam in The Netherlands. While the aircraft was urgently required for the bomber offensive, it was handicapped with a poor operational ceiling and load carrying capability.

The Avro Manchester was designed as a twin-engine heavy bomber capable of carrying loads of 8,000 lb., the prototype flying on 25 July 1939. Production aircraft were delivered to No.207 Squadron from November 1940 and the aircraft conducted its first operational bombing sorties when a force attacked the port of Brest, France, on the night of 24/25 February 1941. The aircraft design was sound, but problems with the Rolls Royce Vulture engines led to it being superseded by the Avro Lancaster after only 209 aircraft had been delivered, production ending in November 1941.

The first production Halifax I, L9485, conducted its maiden flight on 11 October 1940, and deliveries to RAF Bomber Command commenced when No.35 Squadron began receiving Halifax MK.I bombers in November that year, operational missions being flown from March 1941.

The Avro Lancaster prototype, a conversion of a twin-engine Avro Manchester heavy bomber, conducted its maiden flight on 9 January 1941. A new build prototype flew in May 1941, and the first production Lancaster MK.I bomber flew for the first time in October that year. The Lancaster had a huge bomb bay, a tremendous load carrying ability and adequate performance for a heavy bomber of the time and would go, together with the Halifax, to be a stalwart of Bomber Commands strength until the end of the war.

Although the best of the British heavy bombers, the Halifax and the Lancaster, the latter not in service at the time of the high altitude daylight bombing campaign, lacked that said high altitude capability, which would reduce the aircraft's vulnerability to enemy defenses, albeit at the expense of bombing accuracy.

Following the introduction of the Halifax a number of daylight bombing missions were flown. The first of these being a daylight attack on the German port of Kiel, conducted by six Halifax I bombers from No.35 Squadron on 30 June 1941; two of the bombers being lost. As the summer of 1941 wore on Halifax bombers, along with other Bombers of Bomber Command, including the Short Stirling, would also be employed on daylight attacks on the German warships in the French port of Brest, joined by a few Fortress I's of No.90 Squadron.

In July 1941, Bomber Command consisted of 49 Squadrons (some documents adjust this figure slightly depending on the operational status of some squadrons), made up, for the most part, by Handley Page Hamden's, Armstrong Whitworth Whitley's and Vickers Wellington twin engine medium bombers (these types had been re-designated from heavy to medium bombers with the introduction of later heavy types). There were eight Squadrons of the new heavy bombers, four being operational, and eight Squadrons of Bristol Blenheim's, now classified as a light bomber, operating with No.2 Group in the daylight bombing role. The thirty seven available medium and heavy bomber squadrons were tasked with night bombing in accordance with the directive issued on 9 July 1941, but some daylight attacks were launched, notably against the German Battlecruisers docked in Brest Harbour. The eight Blenheim Squadrons would continue daylight attacks on continental fringe and shipping targets operating from medium and low altitudes, often heavily protected by fighters, occasionally venturing further afield to attack targets in Germany. Absent from the above figures was No.90 Squadron and its Fortress I's, which would be employed in an experimental high altitude bombing role, which despite the directive of 9 July, would be conducted mainly against naval targets and port towns, as would much of Bomber Commands night bomber offensive.

2

FORMATION OF 90 SQUADRON AND INTRODUCTION OF THE FORTRESS I (B-17C) TO RAF SERVICE

No.90 Squadron was initially formed as a RFC (Royal Flying Corp) fighter squadron at Shawbury, Shropshire, on 8 October 1917, but was disbanded on 3 August 1918, before reforming again as a RAF Home Defence Fighter unit on the 14th of that month, disbanding again in June 1919. The Squadron reformed in March 1937, this time as a bomber squadron, equipped with Hawker Hind single-engine bi-plane light bombers, receiving Blenheim I twin-engine monoplane bombers from May that year, then, from early 1939, improved Blenheim IV bombers.

On the outbreak of World War II on 3 September 1939, the squadron was mobilised and within days was stood by for operations, but flew no operational missions, becoming to all intents and purposes a training squadron until absorbed by No.17 OTU (Operational Training Unit) in May 1940.

No.90 Squadron reformed at RAF Watton as a bomber unit on 7 May 1941, the first squadron in the RAF to be equipped with the Boeing B-17C Flying Fortress, which was designated Fortress MK.I in RAF service. The Squadron was to be commanded by W/Cdr. J. MacDougall, D.F.C. who was posted from No.101 bomber squadron then based at West Raynham.

The first B-17C (Fortress I), AN521, had arrived at Prestwick, Ayr, Scotland, at 06.11 hours on 14 April (Easter Monday) 1941. The aircraft had been flown to Scotland from Gandar, Newfoundland, by Major Walshe, USAAC, in a crossing which took 8 hours 26 minutes, then the shortest crossing recorded. Records show that AN521 was accompanied by AN534, which then went to Burtonwood, the Boeing MU (Maintenance Unit), AN521 going to RAF Watton where it was flown on (local flying) by Major Walshe on 14 April.

Fortress I AN528 (formerly B-17C SN: 40-2064) on a test flight prior to its delivery to the RAF. USAF

On 30 April, Major Walshe and two other USAAC crew flew the aircraft, and on 3 May Major Walshe took the aircraft up with RAF P/O Roarke for training, which continued the following day, but P/O Roarke subsequently failed his oxygen test at RAE Farnborough and was therefore, posted away from the squadron, landing at 144 Squadron (a Handley Page Hampden unit). The criteria for squadron personnel that crew had to pass an oxygen test lasting 4 hours at 35,000 ft.

On 5 May, squadron personnel began to arrive at Watton in the shape of P/O D.M.G. Robertson, Sgt. Clifford (from 115 Squadron Marham), Sgt. Weil (from 115 Squadron), Sgt. Wills, a Canadian, (from 115 Squadron) and Sgt. Wood, an Australian, (from 115 Squadron). On the 6th, more personnel arrived: F/O J.C.H. Hawley (from 51 Squadron at Dishforth), P/O R.S. Boast (from 35 Squadron at Linton), Sgt. G. Garwood (from 77 Squadron at Topcliffe) and Sgt. T. Imrie (from 51 Squadron at Dishforth). On the 7th, the CO (Commanding Officer), W/Cdr. MacDougall, arrived to take command; other personnel arriving consisting of Sgt. P. Black (from 102 Squadron at Topcliffe), Sgt. H.D.P. Sleath (from 102 Squadron) and Sgt's D.G. Night and Worthington (both from 35 Squadron at Lincoln).

Boeing Fortress MK.I AN529 (formerly B-17C SN: 40-2065) at Hatfield near Prestwick, Ayrshire, Scotland, following its delivery from the United States in May 1941. This aircraft was written off when it was badly damaged in a forced landing near Fort Maddalena, Libya, on 8 November 1941. MAP

On the 7th, Major Walshe (USAAC) flew with RAF crew, F/O Hawley, P/O Robertson and P/O Boast, in Fortress I AN521 to the Boeing MU at Burtonwood. AN521 remained at Burtonwood, the crew returning to Watton in AN534.

On the 8th, the CO, W/Cdr. MacDougall, was given instruction on the Fortress with some 15 minutes flying in the morning and 1 hour 15 minutes in the afternoon. After a few days with the squadron where he had been instructing personnel on the Fortress's turbo superchargers, Mr. Schultz, design engineer for Turbo's at General Electric in the United States, departed for Burtonwood. Aircrew continued to arrive for the squadron; F/Lt. P.D.S. Bennett, D.F.C. arriving from 50 Squadron at Lindholme.

On the 10th, the CO and Major Walshe flew to Massingham where they conducted a series of "circuits and landings" to ascertain whether or not the aerodrome was suitable for the operation of the B-17.

The British Prime Minister, Winston Churchill, in company with other distinguished officials strolls past a Fortress I during a review of Bomber Command aircraft held at West Raynham on 6 June 1941. MAP

On the 11th, Fortress I AN534, crewed by W/Cdr. MacDougall, Major Walshe, F/Lt. Bennett and F/O Hawley, was flown to Burtonwood. Major Walshe and F/O Hawley transferred to AN529 and flew this aircraft to Watton while W/Cdr. MacDougall and F/Lt. Bennett flew AN534 to Bascombe Down in order to obtain information about bombing trials. With the addition of AN529, No.90 Squadron now had a strength of 2 Fortress I's.

Over The next few days aircrew continued to arrive, but much of the ground crew had to be borrowed from No.21 and 82 Squadrons, and a Captain J. Connally Lieutenant Bradley and Sgt. Covington of the USAAC joined the unit for training purposes, arriving from Bascombe Down. On the 12th, No.2 Group Bomber Command, which would oversee Fortress operations, ordered that the

Fortress aircraft be operated from Bodney, a satellite field for Watton, while the personnel would remain billeted at Watton. At 15.00 hours that afternoon 90 Squadrons two Fortress I's were flown to Bodney, piloted by W/Cdr. MacDougall and Major Walshe respectively, where it was found that the aerodrome was unsuitable for the B-17 operations. The CO then went to No.2 Group HQ to report, with the result that the squadron was ordered to move to Massingham, although this was not confirmed until 14 May, circuits and landings being conducted at Bodney on the 13th.

The iconic figure of the British Prime Minister, Winston Churchill, watching a display of a Fortress I flown by Major Walshe (USAAC) during the review of Bomber Command aircraft held at West Raynham on 6 June 1941. MAP

A Fortress I of No.90 Squadron runs its engines at West Raynham, Norfolk, on 20 June 1941. RAF

On the 15th, the squadron moved, personnel to West Raynham, while the aircraft were flown to Massingham, a satellite aerodrome for West Raynham. At 07.30 hours one Fortress flown by Major Walshe and his crew took off for Burtonwood, but abandoned the journey due to poor visibility, landing back at Massingham. W/Cdr. MacDougall and his crew flew direct to West Raynham, then flew to Farnborough for an oxygen test.

American personnel, USAAC and civilian, continued to increase with the arrival of Mr. Crawford, a Boeing engineer. He had arrived in the United Kingdom on 11 April, his journey involving a Clipper to Lisbon, Portugal, then a KLM flight to Bristol. A Mr. Franklyn Joseph had arrived in the UK from America on 11 April and arrived at No.90 Squadron on the 14th of May to instruct crews on the Sperry bombsight.

On the 22nd, a Fortress I was inspected by the Minister of Aircraft Production at West Raynham, followed the next day by a review of Bomber Command aircraft at Abingdon by H.H. King George VI. A Fortress I was present, in company with a variety of other aircraft, including a Handley Page Halifax, Avro Manchester, Short Stirling, Avro Lancaster, Vickers Wellington V and Martin Maryland. The King was accompanied by Princess's Margaret and Elizabeth (the current reigning Monarch in 2014).

On this date one Flight of 90 Squadron was formed, S/Ldr. McLaren arriving from 13 OTU (Operational Training Unit), Bicester, to take command of the Flight, designated O Flight. The following day he took command of his crew.

On 25 May, three Fortress I's, AN521, AN523 and AN527, were collected from Burtonwood and flown to Massingham. This brought the squadron's strength to five Fortress I's, the new aircraft joining AN529 and AN534 already with the squadron. By the following day four complete crews were on strength, three trained for flying without instructor and the other, S/Ldr. McLarens crew, still training.

Crews consisted of:

Captain	W/Cdr. McDougall	S/Ldr. McLaren	F/Lt. Bennett	P/O Hawley
2nd Pilot	Sgt. Wood	P/O Wayman	P/O Mathieson	P/O Robertson
Observer	F/O Skelton	P/O Cotton	P/O Boast	Sgt. Lewis
1st W/Op	F/O Barnes	Sgt. Peggs	Sgt. Davies	Sgt. Willis
2nd W/O	Sgt. Imrie	Sgt. Weil	Sgt. James	Sgt. Garwood
AG	Sgt. Danby	Sgt. Worthington	Sgt. Allan	Sgt. Knight
AG	Sgt. Clifford		Sgt. Willis	Sgt. Blacklow

Flying training continued on the 27th, on which date W/Cdr. MacDougall and his crew flew a Fortress to Polebrook aerodrome to inspect it from the air.

Three more USAAC personnel, a Colonel and two Majors, arrived at the squadron from Burtonwood, for a visit. The assistance from the Americans was warmly welcomed as the squadron infrastructure was taking shape amidst crew and material shortages. For their part, the Americans themselves, those visiting and those assigned to the squadron, had a deep interest in the squadron as it strived to become operational, as the squadrons operational lessons would be absorbed by the USAAC. The three visitors departed on the 39th, leaving the American contingent at the pilots and three Sgt. Ground staff.

On 30 May the new Fortress I's that had arrived on the 25th were given an inspection as no record of previous flying had come with them. The Fortress I that had been at Bascombe Down for bombing trials was sent to West Raynham for several days to be inspected, before returning to Bascombe Down, where it landed at 15.00 hours on 1 June 1941.

AGRAMATIC SKETCH OF
OEING AIRCRAFT N°AN 528
OESTROYED BY FIRE AT
POLEBROOK 3-7-41 SHOWING
POSITIONS OF ENGINES AND
WIND DIRECTION.

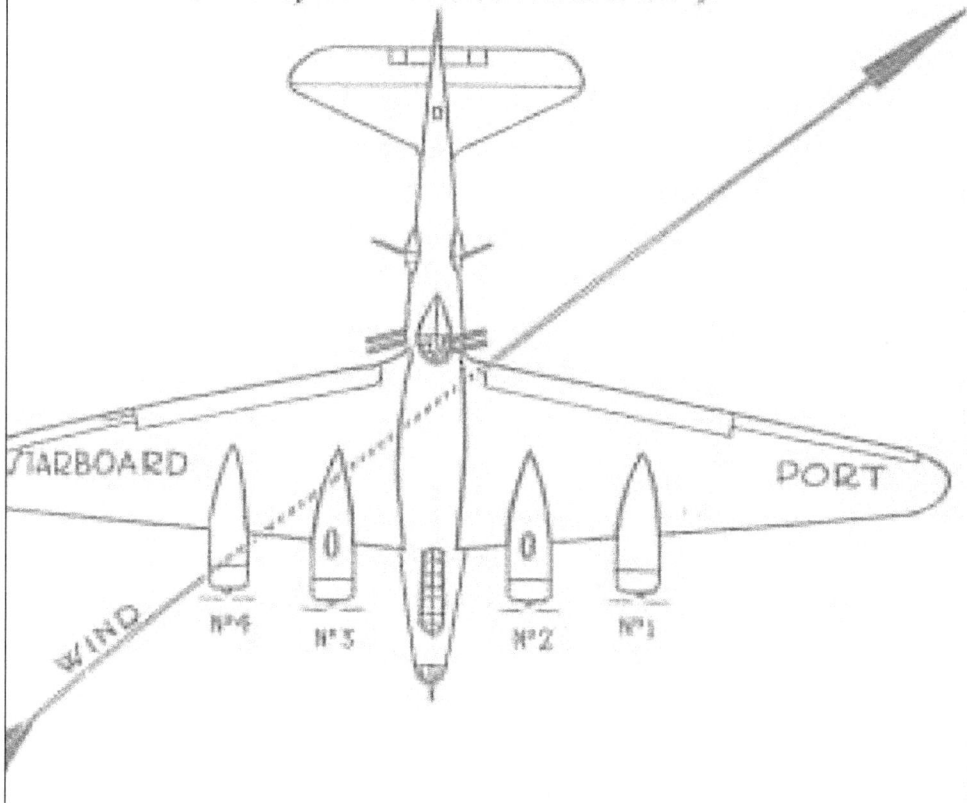

STARBOARD

PORT

WIND

N°4   N°3   N°2   N°1

Previous page: Diagrammatic sketch showing the wind direction and the engines of Fortress AN528 which was destroyed by fire on 3 July 1941. National Archives

This page: Two views of the burnt out hulk of AN528 following the fire on 3 July 1941. National Archives

On 3 June 1941, a Fortress, flown by F/Lt. Bennet, with three additional crews aboard, flew to Burtonwood to collect three more Fortress I's. The four Fortress's departed Burtonwood from 19.00 hours. The first two aircraft, flown by Captain Connally (USAAC) and Lt. Bradley (USAAC), landed at Massingham at 20.00 hours, but the other two aircraft were unable to land at Massingham due to very low could that had socked in before their arrival, F/Lt. Bennet landing at Coningsby and F/O Hawley landing at Sutton Bridge, both flying to Massingham the following day.

On the 4th, a Fortress I, W/Cdr. MacDougall and crew, reached 38,000 ft. during an altitude test, the height being reached in 40 minutes, at which time the aircraft was still climbing at 500 ft. per minute. It was noted during the test, due to imperfections in the equipment, the crew were feeling the effects of the altitude. The tests, which included oxygen and wireless equipment altitude tests, were conducted while Air Commodore Kelly, Group Signals personnel and representatives from the RAE (Royal Aircraft Establishment) were present at West Raynham (Massingham). Following the test flight W/Cdr. MacDougall flew to Farnborough for a post-test conference.

On 6 June, there was a review of Bomber Command aircraft held at West Raynham, attended by the Prime Minister, the Rt. Hon. Winston Churchill and other officials, including Air Marshall Sir W. Sholto-Douglas, K.C.B., M.D., D.F.C. A Fortress I was present, along with Halifax, Stirling, Manchester and Wellington II aircraft, a fly-past taking place after the inspection; the Fortress I being flown by Major Walshe and Captain Connally (USAAC).

The next week or so consisted of training and stand-downs, but on the 14th a Fortress I with W/Cdr. MacDougall and crew and Major Walshe (USAAC), flew to Swanton Morley where the aircraft was inspected by Sir Archibald Sinclair, Minister of State for Air.

On 22 June 1941, the Squadron suffered its first casualties with the Fortress when AN522 crashed. The aircraft, crewed by F/O Hawley, Lt. Bradley (USAAC), Sgt. Black, Sgt. Garwood, Sgt. Willis, S/Ldr. Robson (Squadron MO - Medical Officer), and F/Lt. Steward (MO for RAE Farnborough), had taken off at on an altitude test at 14.30 hours. The squadron was informed at 18.00 hours that a Fortress had crashed some 10 miles north of Catterick; all of the crew were killed except F/Lt. Steward who stated that the Fortress had been flying at 33,000 ft. when it entered cumulus cloud. Heavy ice began to form and hailstones as large as "golf balls" began to enter the aircraft through the open gun ports. The squadron records then state **"The pilot appeared to lose control and the aircraft went into a T.V. dive. At 25,000 ft. the port wing broke off and the fuselage broke into two pieces. F/Lt. Steward was in the rear part of the fuselage which fell at a slower rate than the other piece, and he was able to abandon ship at a height believed to be about 12,000 ft. and make a parachute descent."**

This Fortress MK.I, AN521 (WP-K), from No.90 Squadron is undergoing an engine change in June 1941. RAF

On 23 June, AN519 was flown to Burtonwood by S/Ldr. McLaren and F/Lt. Bennet for long range fuel tanks to be fitted. On this date the squadron was stood by for what would have been its first operational mission – to fly Sir Stafford Cripps, British Ambassador the USSR, to Archangel, USSR. However, the following day the squadron received an order that the flight had been cancelled.

On the 26th, W/Cdr. MacDougall flew to Polebrook aerodrome, Northhamtonshire, which was again inspected to determine its suitability for Fortress operations. The following day the squadron commenced its move to Polebrook, the advance party departing West Raynham by road. On the 28th, two Fortress I's, AN519 and AN523, flew to Polebrook; three other Fortress's, AN526, AN527 and AN528, arriving on the 29th; AN529 remaining at West Raynham as it was unserviceable. On the 29th, AN519 flew from Polebrook to Burtonwood to collect spares, calling in at West Raynham on the return journey to deliver parts for AN529, which was rendered serviceable and flown to Polebrook on 1 July 1941.

On 30 June, No.90 Squadron took over control of Ashton bombing range from No.17 OTU, the latter based at Upwood. A new pyramid shape target some 20 square yards by 30 square yards was built as the aim point for the squadron's high level bombing with the Sperry Mk 0-1 bomb sight.

On 3 July, the squadron lost another aircraft when Fortress I AN528 burnt out after an engine caught fire while the aircraft was being run by ground crew at 23.00 hours.

The bombing training produced mixed results for the squadron. Only two bombs were dropped on the 3 July and 10 on the 4th; average error on the 4th being 200 yards, a deterioration from the 150 yards achieved on the 2nd. Ten bombs dropped during the morning of the 5th, average error being down to 95 yards, credited to better bombing conditions. In the afternoon only 4 bombs were dropped as cloud closed in. Up until now bombing had been conducted from 10,000 ft., but on the 6th the program called for bombing from 10,000 and 20,000 ft., only one bomb being dropped (undetermined height), during the first sortie by P/O Mathieson and crew at 13.30 hours due to the aircraft having a faulty bomb sight. At 14.15 hours W/Cdr. MacDougall and crew took off for bombing practice over the Ashton range; four bombs being dropped each at 10,000 ft. and 20,000 ft. On the 7th, P/O Mathieson and crew took off at 05.00 hours and dropped fifteen practice bombs on Ashton range, average error being some 200 yards, although the closest bomb to the target had an error of only 22 yards.

Of note is the fact that the highest altitude bombing practice for the squadron was 20,000 ft., while within days the squadron was to bomb operational targets from altitudes in excess of 30,000.ft.

3

FORTRESS I HIGH ALTITUDE BOMBING CAMPAIGN, NORTH WEST EUROPE – JULY TO SEPTEMBER 1941

For No.90 Squadron, 7 July 1941 was used to prepare for the squadrons, and the Fortress I's, first operational mission in World War II. The squadrons Battle Order No.1, issued on the 7th, called for three Fortress I's, AN526, AN519 and AN529, each to be armed with 4 x 1,100 lb. American demolition bombs, to be operationally ready by "pm" on the 7th in preparation for the first mission scheduled to be flown the following day.

The Fortress I's introduction to operations in World War II commenced at 15.00 hours on 8 July 1941 when three aircraft, AN526 (G) (W/Cdr. MacDougall, Sgt. Wood, F/O Skelton, F/O Barnes, Sgt. Imrie, Sgt. Danby and Sgt. Clifford), AN519 (H) (S/Ldr. McLaren, P/O Wayman, P/O Boast, Sgt. Peggs, Sgt. Neil, Sgt. Street and Sgt. Jones) and AN529 (C) (P/O Mathieson, Sgt. Sleath, Sgt. Lewis, Sgt. Davies, Sgt. James, Sgt. Wells and Sgt. Allan), took off from Polebrook to conduct a planned high altitude attack on the German port of Wilhelmshaven in North West Germany; the centre of attack to be the Submarine Building Docks.

The plan of attack was for the three aircraft to fly out in open formation and bomb the target from an altitude of 27,000 ft. then climb to 31,000 - 32,000 ft. on the flight out from the target area. AN526 bombed the target; AN529, having two bombs hung up, required two runs at the target, but was still only able to release two of its four bombs. It should be noted that report W.P. (41) 160 dated 10 July 1941 states that the bombs were dropped on the "Naval Barracks at Willhelmshaven... which were seen to explode directly on the targets, which lie in a thickly populated part of the town."

Map of Western Europe including the British Isles and Norway, the main areas of operation for the Fortress I in 1941. NZTEC

On the way out to the target AN519 had suffered engine problems at 20,000 ft. during its climb out from base; the trouble found to be "oil leaking from the breather valves of all four engines." When the aircraft attained an altitude of 27,000 ft. the oil was still leaking out and covering the tail plane where it froze, estimated at that time to be about 1 inch thick. Crew members reported "severe vibrations" and the pilot could not get the aircraft to climb any higher and pressure was falling off at a rapid rate, therefore, S/Ldr. McLaren decided it was best to abandon the primary target, attacking Norderney on the Frisian Islands instead; all four bombs missing the town.

Copy of No.90 Squadrons Battle Order No.1 dated 7 July 1941. National Archives

AN529 (C), still with two bombs hung up, attempted to drop these on targets in the Frisian Islands on the return home, but the bombs wouldn't budge, therefore the aircraft turned for home. A short time later, at an altitude of 27,000 ft., the aircraft began to vibrate severely for a period of 14 minutes; the wireless operators keys breaking up. During the first four minutes the aircraft lost 12,000 ft. in altitude, now flying at 15,000 ft. with broadband IFF switched on. The vibrations ceased at 14,000 ft. and the frozen oil on the tail plane which had increased in thickness, began to thaw and the aircraft safely returned to base. Nome of the three Fortress I's were subjected to anti-aircraft fire or attacks by enemy fighters, although the crew of AN526 reported Me.109 fighters north of Terschelling.

AN519 (H) landed back at base at 18.35 hours followed by AN529 (C), which landed at 19.00 hours, with AN526 (G) landing at 19.05 hours, bringing to an end the first operational mission with the Fortress I during World War II.

The No.90 Squadron narrative of the attack is reproduced below verbatim:

"**Aircraft G and C attacked the primary target between 1650 and 1700 hours from 28,000 and 30,000 feet respectively.**

Aircraft G dropped 4 x 1100 lb. demolition bombs and aircraft C had 2 x 1100 lb. bombs hang up and only two were released. Two bursts were observed on the target and a stick of four bombs was seen with the first bomb 250 yards west of BAUHAFEN and the others 150 yard intervals to the S.E. Electrical failure of both cameras prevented photographs being taken. The astrodome in aircraft G froze up at 18,000 feet and made fire control impossible. 2 E/A believed to be ME109's were seen 40 miles north of TERSCHELLING at 30,000 ft., 2,000 feet below our aircraft. They climbed and approached on the starboard beam closing to about 600 - 800 yards when one of them appeared to go into an involuntary spin and was seen still spinning about 600 feet below. The second aircraft broke off the attack and followed the first one down. No fire was exchanged.

Aircraft H experienced loss of oil at 28,000 feet and abandoned primary task, attacking NORDENEY from this height at 1645 hours. 4 x 1100 lb. bombs were dropped and bursts were seen on the sand about 500 yards from the town. Photographs were taken of NORDENEY (but the bomb bursts were not shown). Lateral flutter due to oil freezing on the tail plane and building up about 7" thick, and consequent vibration experienced after bombing. This was eventually overcome by losing height to 15,000 feet at which height the oil thawed and cleared the tail plane. All four airscrews were feathered in succession but this had no apparent effect on the vibration."

There was no operational flying over the next few days, but non-operational test and training flights continued with 2 altitude test sorties on 10 July and an altitude test on AN523 and turbo test at high altitude on AN526 on the 11th.

An operation was planned for 14 July, three Fortress I's, AN526, AN523 and AN529, being made ready on the 13th, aircraft dispersed for 17.00 hours and then bombed up. At 07.00 hours on the 14th, the three crews reported to the crew rooms, but the operation was cancelled at 08.30 hours after reports of adverse weather over the planned ingress route to the target. In the afternoon the operational crews reported back as the operation was expected to be re-scheduled for the following day. However, as adverse weather was expected on the 15th the operation could not be carried out. Operations were planned several times over the next week, all being cancelled due to adverse weather.

Non-operational flying continued with an altitude test on AN526, flown by Captain Connally (USAAC) and crew. Captain Connally also flew new pilots on 2 hours local flying and landings. On the 15th, adverse weather meant only a single non-operational sortie was flown, Captain Connally taking new pilots up for local flying and landings. A similar program of local flying and landing practice for new pilots, under the tutelage of Captain Connally, was conducted on the 16th, 2 flights being conducted at 10.30 and 16.00 hours. On the 17th, one sortie was flown at 07.40 hours, Captain Connally taking off with new pilots for local flying and landing practice. There was no flying on the 18th, but training sorties continued on the 19th, Captain Connally taking off at 11.05 hours with new pilots for local flying and landing practice. At 14.30 hours S/Ldr. McLaren took off with new pilots and wireless operators for local flying lasting 45 minutes and at 15.15 hours Major Walshe (USAAC) took off with new pilots for local flying and landings lasting 2 hours and Captain Connally took off at 17.45 hours with new pilots for local flying and landings.

The MK.10A oxygen system was tested on AN530 on 21 July 1941, and the following day W/Cdr. MacDougall and crew took the aircraft up on an altitude oxygen test, reaching 38,000 ft., which was held for 20 minutes, oxygen supply being deemed satisfactory.

Copy of No.90 Squadrons Battle Order No.1 dated 13 July 1941. This mission was cancelled. National Archives

No.90 Squadrons second operational mission was conducted on 23 July 1941. Three Fortress I's, AN530 (F) (W/Cdr. MacDougall, Sgt. Wood, F/O Skelton, F/O Barnes, Sgt. Imrie, Sgt. Danby and Sgt. Clifford), AN523 (D) (S/Ldr. McLaren, P/O Wayman, P/O Boast, Sgt. Peggs, Sgt. Weil, Sgt. Street and Sgt. Jones) and AN529 (C) F/Lt. Mathieson, Sgt. Sleath, Sgt. Lewis, Sgt. Davies, Sgt. James, Sgt. Willis and Sgt. Allan), took off between 08.57 and 09.02 hours to attack Berlin.

When about 60 miles from the Danish Coast AN530 (W/Cdr. MacDougall) turned back as he was not able to maintain height. The other two Fortress's crossed the Danish coast flying inland for some 58 miles before abandoning the mission as condensation trials were forming at an altitude of 32,000 ft. AN530 landed at 12.21 hours followed by the other two aircraft at 12.35; all three aircraft returning with their bomb loads of 4 x 1,100 lb. demolition bombs.

The Following day the same three aircraft and crews took off between 11.20 and 11.30 hours to conduct a high altitude attack on the German Navy 11-in gun Battlecruiser *Gneisenau* and the 8-in gun Heavy Cruiser *Prinz Eugen* in harbor at Brest, France, in support of a daylight attack by 15 Halifax bombers from No.35 and 76 Squadrons carrying 2,000 lb. armour piercing bombs. Around the same time the 11-gun Battlecruiser *Scharnhorst*, moored at La Pallice, was attacked by Halifax bombers, which dropped 25 tons of H.E bombs, at least one bomb being claimed to have hit the ship. These powerful German warships were a thorn in Admiralty's side with the threat of a break out into the Atlantic where they could wreak havoc with Britain's lifeline, the Atlantic convoys bringing in food stuffs, raw materials and war materials.

Scharnhorst, previously berthed at Brest with her sister ship *Gneisenau*, had departed Brest around 10 pm on 21 July bound for La Pallice, some 270 miles south of Brest (depending on route), where she was to conduct post refit trials. She was located at La Pallice by a Supermarine Spitfire reconnaissance aircraft on the morning of 23 July. Later that day four Short Stirling heavy bombers attacked the warship at La Pallice with 2,000 lb. bombs; one Stirling being shot down by fighters of 1./JG 2 with 2 Me.109 fighters being claimed shot down by the bomber gunners. During the course of the night of 23/24 July, a force of 25 Whitley's from Bomber Command and 7 Beauforts from Coastal Command attacked the *Scharnhorst* at La Pallice. The attacks at La Pallice resulted in damage being inflicted on the *Scharnhorst* by several direct and indirect hits resulting in her returning to Brest for repairs.

Operation orders called for the Fortress I's to be over the target at 14.00 hours, the aircraft dropping their respective loads of 4 x 1,100 lb. bombs, between 14.06 and 14.10 hours; aircraft AN530 and AN523 bombing from an altitude of 30,000 ft. with AN529 bombing from 32,000 ft. Bombs were reported bursting "on the torpedo station along the side of the quay at RADE ABRI and on the outer corner of the dry dock." The Fortress's were subjected to flak, reported as fairly accurate, but about 1,000 ft. below and behind the formation. On the way out from the target, at 14.15 hours, a pair of single-engine fighters were noted quite a distance from the bombers. Then 3 aircraft, identified as Me.109 fighters, started to climb towards the bombers, but were lost from view and no interception took place. The three aircraft returned to base, AN529 landing at 15.30 followed by AN530 and AN523 landing at 15.45.

The attack on Brest by the Halifax bombers achieved limited success, a number of hits being recorded, but at the cost of five bombers lost. The attacks on the German warships and diversionary attacks on targets in Cherbourg included 149 Bomber Command sorties, the highest number flown in daylight since the outbreak of war; 9 Blenheim bombers from Coastal Command also attacking the railway centre at Hazebrouck, and 529 Fighter Command sorties being flown in support of the operations. As well as claimed hits on warships - *Gneisenau* was claimed to have been hit 7 times - bombs fell on the docks at Brest and in the town and docks of Cherbourg. From all the raids that day the RAF lost sixteen bombers and 8 fighters, claiming 21 German fighters destroyed, 7 probably destroyed and 9 damaged by bomber gunners and 12 destroyed, 5 probably destroyed and 5 damaged by British fighters. It should be noted that these claims for German fighters destroyed were vastly overstated as were Germans claims that two Fortress's were shot down by 3./JG 2, which were inaccurate and may have been other aircraft.

Previous Page: Crew of a Fortress I of 90 Squadron put on their electrically heated flying suites at Polebrook as they prepare for a high altitude attack on the German Battlecruiser *Gneisenau* at Brest, France, on 24 July 1941. RAF

Above: The German Battlecruisers *Scharnhorst* and *Gneisenau* docked at Brest took up much of Bomber Commands effort during 1941. The German warships were subjected to day and night attack by Bomber Command and Coastal Command aircraft including Armstrong Whitworth Whitley, Handley Page Halifax and Fortress I bombers from the former and Bristol Beaufort bombers from the latter. The above photograph was taken during a daylight attack on Brest by bombers from No.3, 4 and 5 Groups RAF Bomber Command. RAF

Crew board a Fortress I of No.90 Squadron at Polebrook on 24 July 1941. The aircraft was part of a force detailed to attack the German Battlecruiser *Gneisenau* **in Brest Harbour.** RAF

At 06.30 hours on 25 July crews were briefed for a planned high altitude attack on Hamburg, Germany, with Emden, Germany, as the secondary target; the mission planned for the following day. The primary aim point for the two Fortress's scheduled to bomb was a railway junction in Hamburg.

The following morning the crews for the days operation reported to the CO, W/Cdr. MacDougall, at 04.30 hours, busying themselves with preparations for the mission which commenced at 07.30 hours, when two Fortress I's, AN530 (F) (F/L.t Matheison, Sgt. Sleath, Sgt. Lewis, Sgt. Davies, Sgt. James, Sgt. Willis and Sgt. Allan) and AN529 (C) (Sgt. Wood, P/O Stokes, P/O Cotton, F/Lt.

Meyer, Sgt. Imrie, Sgt. Danby and Sgt. Clifford), took off for the high altitude attack on Hamburg, with Bremen added as a secondary target alongside Emden. This was Sgt. Wood's first mission as captain of a Fortress, having previously flown as the second pilot.

The official caption for the above photograph states that the crew is climbing out of Fortress MK.I WP-G (this code was allocated to AN526) after an attack on the German Battlecruiser *Gneisenau*. However, operational records show that AN526 took part only in the first Fortress I operation on 8 July 1941; the target being the German port of Wilhelmshaven in North West Germany. RAF

AN529 (C), at an altitude of 30,000 ft., turned back when in position 53 degrees 30' N. 04 degrees 30 E. over the North Sea due to adverse weather, 10/10ths cloud cover and thunderstorms. The aircraft landed back at base, with its load of 4 x 1,100 lb. demolition bombs, at 09.30 hours.

The other Fortress, AN530 (F), abandoned the primary target when in position 53 degrees 30' N. 07 degrees, 30' E. due to "masses of cumulo-nimbus with tops up to 30,000 feet, and heavy thunderstorms." The aircraft then headed for Emden which was bombed, the 4 x 1,100 lb. demolition bombs being released at an altitude of 32,000 feet. The crew observed bomb bursts in the N.W. section of the town. There was no noted anti-aircraft fire or enemy fighters, but on the return journey the aircraft experienced trouble with No's 1 and 2 engines, the Captain opting to make a forced landing at Horsham St. Faith at 11.50 hours.

On 26 July a new squadron CO, W/Cdr. P.F. Webster, arrived on the 26th to take over command of the squadron from W/Cdr. MacDougall, but there were no more operations in July, although one Fortress was destroyed and the crew killed when the aircraft crashed shortly after taking off for an altitude test flight at 17.00 hours on the 28th. The previous day a Fortress I had been collected from Horsham and another from Burtonwood.

As noted above, the squadron lost its third Fortress, AN534, when the aircraft, which had taken off at 17.00 hours for an altitude climb test, crashed shortly afterwards. The crew, all of whom were killed, consisted of Sgt. Brooks (1st Pilot), Lt. Hendricks (USAAC - Note: the USAAC changed to the USAA Force in June 1941, but for several months units and detachments continued to be administered under the USAAC) 2nd Pilot, F/Sgt. Muir, Sgt. Pugh, Sgt. Henderson, Sgt. Smith and Sgt. Bradley. At the time of the crash AN534 had been modified with the MK.X Oxygen system and de-froster panels on the aircraft windows. The aircraft had undergone a 100 hour inspection on the 19th.

The following extracts are from the Court of Inquiry Witness Statements for the Fortress I loss on 28 July 1941:

Mrs. D.M. Alexander

"I was working in a field next to the one into which the aircraft ultimately crashed. I heard the sound of an aircraft overhead and looked up, at first, I saw nothing, but then the aircraft came out of the cloud and I saw that it was a four engine aircraft. It came out of cloud at about an angle of 45 degrees, I did not then think that there was anything wrong, the aircraft then went into a steeper dive facing straight at me. I thought that the pilot was stunting until the dive became practically vertical when a piece of the aircraft came away, then she lurched away from me, burst into flames and went straight into a spiral, and the next moment hit the ground with the engines still going. I ran straight to the spot but there were flames and black smoke and flares going off and small explosions, and it was impossible to be of any assistance."

Mr. Pettigrew…

"I was on duty on K.3 Observer post when I first had a plot towards the east at grid square 3709 at about 3,000 ft. The plane which was identifiable as four engine appeared to be holding a normal course towards K.3 but immediately after being sighted entered cloud. The plane approached and passed overhead travelling in a westerly direction towards grid square 2109, Plane was invisible from original sighting until its emergence at 2109 approximately 1 to 2 miles from K.3, at about 2,000 feet in a vertical dive. After travelling about one third of the distance toward ground the right wing as seen from K.3 began to break up. About four pieces, one being larger than the others were observed. About another third of the way down flames appeared at the nose of the aircraft, and immediately enveloped the whole machine. Upon crashing there were two muffled explosions and a column of black smoke appeared."

This witness added that visibility at the time was about 3 to 5 miles and cloud cover about 8/10ths.

The following is an extract from the log in Observer Post K.3:

"1710 Plane passed overhead flying in westerly direction, not seen, obscured by cloud. First seen in direction of 2109 1 - 2 miles from post disintegrating in air, and diving straight to earth, crashed less than one minute after passing overhead. Observer Pettigrew sent to scene of accident on Centres instructions but military were already on the spot and would not give any information."

Finding of the Court of Inquiry into the crash of Fortress, AN534:

"We find from the evidence that the following facts have been established:

(i)   The aircraft broke up due to structural failure during attempted recovery from a high speed dive.

(ii) The aircraft caught fire after the structural failure.

(iii) The cause of the dive cannot be determined but it is assumed that the cause was due to:-

        (a) Faulty Instrument Flying

                    OR

        (b) Incorrect engagement of the automatic pilot.

The only other Fortress I flying by 90 Squadron during July 1941 was an altitude test on the 27th, Catterick - Prestwick; 38,000 ft. being attained, the aircraft landing at Polebrook at 20.00 hours, and a single training sortie on the 30th and 2 training flights on the 31st.

Three of a Fortress I's load of 4 x 1,100 lb. demolition bombs falling to earth near Kiel, Germany, on 2 August 1941. The bombs were released some three miles from the aim point at an altitude of 33,000 ft. RAF

Two Fortress I's, AN540 (F) (P/O Sturmey, P/O Franks, P/O Boast, F/Sgt. Goldsmith, Sgt. Needle, Sgt. Ambose and Sgt. Birtwhistle) and AN529 (C) (S/Ldr. Matheison, Sgt. Sleath, Sgt. Lewis, Sgt. Davis, Sgt. James, Sgt. Willis and Sgt. Allan), took off between 14.38 and 14.41 hours on 2 August to conduct a high altitude attack on Kiel under 2 Group Operational Orders. AN530 (F), which took off first, took up formation with a training aircraft by mistake and once the mistake had been realised the aircraft was unable to locate the other Fortress, and, therefore, returned to base, landing at 15.15 hours. The remaining Fortress continued with the mission, and at 17.35 hours, dropped its load of 4 x 1,100 lb. demolition bombs on Kiel from an altitude of 33,000 ft. The crew did not observe the bomb bursts, but did note smoke columns rising south of Kiel Fjord. No enemy fighters were encountered en-route to or from or over the target and no flak was noted. The Fortress returned to base and landed at 19.40 hours.

At 17.15 hours Fortress I AN530 (F), with the same crew as earlier, took off to conduct a high altitude attack on Emden. Thickening cloud was encountered over the Frisian Islands and it was therefore decided to bomb Borkum in the Frisian Islands, the 4 x 1,100 lb. demolition bombs being released at an altitude of 32,000 ft. On the return journey, when about 20 miles N.W. of Texel at 20.20 hours, the Fortress was attacked by 2 Me.109F's when at an altitude of 22,000 ft. The German fighters pressed home attacks, hitting the Fortress in several areas, although only minor damage was inflicted with no casualties among the crew. The crew report stated that the German fighters broke off the attacks after one was hit in the engine by the Fortress defensive guns, the Fortress continuing on its homeward journey, landing back at base at 21.05 hours.

On 6 August No.90 Squadron was tasked with a high altitude attack on the German Battlecruisers *Scharnhorst* and *Gneisenau* lying in Brest harbor. Two Fortress I's, AN529 (C) (S/Ldr Mathieson, Sgt. Sleath, Sgt. Lewis, Sgt. Davis, Sgt. James, Sgt. Willis and Sgt. Allan) and AN523 (D) (P/O Sturmey, P/O Franks, P/O Boast, F/Sgt. Goldsmith, Sgt. Needle, Sgt. Ambrose and Sgt. Birtwhistle), took off between 06.38 and 06.40 hours. Being airborne within a few minutes of each other, both aircraft headed to the target in company, but conducted their attacks separately from different altitudes. The first, AN529 (C), was at 33,000 ft. when it reached the target area, but had to abandon any hopes of conducting "a proper bombing run" as ice had formed on the bomb sight. Instead the aircraft's load of 4 x 1,100 lb. demolition bombs was jettisoned over the docks, bomb bursts being noted on the shore and the Rade Abri mooring's area. The other Fortress, AN523 (D), conducted its bomb run and released its 4 x 1,100 lb. demolition bombs from at altitude of 32,000 ft., bomb bursts being noted in the Rade Abri.

During the attack the aircraft encountered only inaccurate light anti-aircraft fire and no enemy aircraft were noted, which was fortunate as the twin upper and two lower guns of AN529 (C) had frozen when the aircraft was at 33,000 ft. and the air gunners could not clear them.

Both aircraft returned to base, AN529 landing at 10.41 hours and AN523 landing at 11.05 hours.

The next mission did not take place until 12 August when four Fortress I's were tasked to support a low level attack on power stations near Cologne, Germany, by Blenheim IV light bombers of No.2 Group. This operation would involve "the heaviest daylight bombing raid against Germany since the outbreak of war", involving some 78 bomber and 485 fighter sorties. The targets for the main force of 54 Blenheim IV light bombers was the Goldenburg, Knapsack power stations near Cologne in the Rhineland.

The Fortress I's were to attack de Koy aerodrome near Cologne and targets in Emden in an attempt to draw off enemy fighters from the main force of 54 Blenheim IV's, the latter being escorted part of the way by several squadrons of Supermarine Spitfire and Westland Whirlwind fighters, other fighter squadrons tasked to meet them on the return home. There were also a few small scale diversion bombing operations on fringe continental targets and large scale fighter sweeps designed to draw enemy attention away from the main force of Blenheim's.

No.90 Squadrons part in the operation commenced at 09.00 hours when Fortress I AN523 (D) (P/O Sturmey, P/O Franks, P/O Boast, P/O Mulligan, Sgt. Needle, F/Sgt. Goldsmith, Sgt. Ambrose and Sgt. Birtwhistle) took off and headed for its target. This aircraft was followed by AN529 (C) (Sgt. Wood, Sgt. Hindshaw, Sgt. Sutton, Sgt. Danby, Sgt. Imrie, Sgt. Timlin and Sgt. Clifford), which took off at 09.40 hours in company with AN532 (J) (P/O Wyman, P/O McDonald, P/O Cotton, Sgt. Peggs, Sgt. Weil, Sgt. Street and Sgt. Jones). The last of the four Fortress I's, AN536 (M) (P/O Taylor, P/O Hart, Sgt. Corbert, Sgt. Brown, Sgt. Honey, Sgt. Williams and Sgt. Merrille), took off at 10.03 hours.

The first of the Fortress I's, AN523, attacked the aerodrome at De Koy, dropping its load of 4 x 1,100 lb. demolition bombs from an altitude of 32,000 ft. Results could not be observed due to cloud cover over the target following bomb release. Following the bomb run the aircraft turned for home having encountered no anti-aircraft fire or enemy fighters.

Fortress I AN529 suffered an unserviceable exhaust pipe on the No.2 engine which caused the supercharger to fail resulting in the sortie being abandoned when the aircraft was at 14,000 ft. near Oxford. The aircraft returned to base with its 4 x 1,100 lb. bombs, landing at 10.45 hours.

On reaching Cologne AN532 dropped its load of 4 x 1,100 lb. bombs from an altitude of 34,000 ft. on a built up area as the primary target was obscured by cloud. Only one of the bombs released properly, three hanging up before releasing late.

AN536 dropped its 4 x 1,100 lb. bombs on Emden, bombing on estimated time of arrival as the target was clouded over during the bomb run. As with the other aircraft no flak or fighters were encountered.

AN523 landed back at base at 11.25 hours, AN532 landed at 13.23 and AN536 landed at 13.50 hours.

The Blenheim operation, made up of 54 Blenheim IV's from No.18, 21, 107, 114, 139 and 226 Squadrons, successfully bombed their targets, but lost 12 of their number to enemy defenses.

Flak bursts fill the sky as a Blenheim IV light bomber of No.2 Group Bomber Command egress's the target after dropping bombs on the Goldenburg power station, Knapsack near Cologne, Germany, on 12 August 1941. RAF

The next Fortress I operation took place on 16 August 1941, when two aircraft, AN532 (J) (P/O Wayman, P/O McDonald, P/O Cotton, Sgt. Peggs, Sgt. Weil, Sgt. Street and Sgt. Jones) and AN525 (D) (P/O Sturmey, P/O Franks, P/O Mulligan, F/Sgt. Goldsmith, Sgt. Needle, Sgt. Ambrose and Sgt. Leahy), took off at 09.03 hours to attack the German Battlecruisers *Scharnhorst* and *Gneisenau* in Brest Harbour.

The first to attack was AN532, which dropped 4 x 1,100 lb. demolition bombs from an altitude of 35,000 ft., results being unobserved due to cloud cover. No fighters were noted, the aircraft encountering only "slight" anti-aircraft fire. This aircraft then returned to Polebrook where it landed at 12.55 hours.

The crew of the second aircraft, AN523, was not so lucky. This aircraft, a short time after the first Fortress, dropped its 4 x 1,100 lb. bombs from an altitude of 32,000 ft., results being unobserved due to the fore mentioned cloud cover. While outbound from the target this aircraft was attacked by seven German fighters described as 5 x Me.109F's and "2 ME 113s". These latter aircraft obviously being misidentified. It is assumed that the report should have read He.113's, which were still being erroneously reported in encounters with RAF aircraft well into 1941. German records show that he attacking German fighters were Me.109F's from 1./JG-2.

The official report of the incident states that the "upper backward firing gun" of the Fortress was unserviceable. In the first firing passes by the German fighters the wireless operator and two back gunners were wounded. The German fighters harried the Fortress from high altitude, the pilot losing height and flying evasive manoeuvres as he could not climb. The attacks continued and the Fortress, which had descended to 6,000 ft., was badly damaged with the English coast nearby.

Due to the damage to the aircraft and on-board casualties, the pilot opted to make an emergency landing at Roborough, Plymouth, but the aircraft overshot on the landing and caught fire when it halted at 11.45 hours. Three of the crew had been killed and a fourth wounded.

The following report on the operations of AN525 on 16 August has been reproduced verbatim. Note the date of 15 August on the documents is a misprint and should read 16 August:

SECRET.

REPORT ON OPERATIONS BY FORTRESS A.N.525 OF 90 SQUADRON ON BREST, 15TH AUGUST, 1941.

Preliminary.

Crew:-

P/O STURMEY...	1st PILOT.
P/O FRANKS	2nd PILOT.
P/O MULLIGAN	OBSERVER.
F/SGT. GOLDSMITH ...	FIRE CONTROLLER.
SGT. NEEDLE ...	W/OP. AG.
SGT. AMBROSE ...	AG. (Side guns)
SGT. LEAHY ...	AG. (Under guns)

Target:- GNEISENAU and/or SCHARNHORST at BREST.

N. S. I. MUD857

CALL SIGN:- 6 A.M. – D.

ACCOUNT OF FLIGHT FROM BASE TO TARGET, INCLUDING BOMBING.

The aircraft set course from POLEBROOK at 0903 hours. The treck followed before crossing the English coast was BASE – OXFORD – GLASTONBURY – illegible 3 miles West of LYME REGIS. The aircraft crossed the Coast NORTH WEST of BREST in company with another Fortress (Captain:- P/O WEYMAN: N. S. I. MUD 466.)

Before taking off, P/O STURMEY had said that he did not think his aircraft would fly above 32,000 ft. and he now found that it would not do so. Mud 466 could and did fly higher and as the two aircraft neared the FRENCH COAST, say at 15 miles NORTH of PLOUDALMEZEAU MUD 466 appeared to be about 3,000 feet above MUD 857 as well as being about 6 miles ahead and up to 30 miles to starboard.

MUD 857 had started making condensation trails at 25,000 feet and these trails continued without intermission until after the target had been bombed. The lowest temperature recorded was about - 30° C. On the outward flight over the sea, all MUD 857's guns had been tested but the front gun would not fire, nor would the upper backward-firing guns.

At about this time an enemy "Y" report (presumably from a Reporting Ship off the N. Coast of France) was intercepted. "4 engine a/c were North of the ship flying very high with vapour trails. A/C ordered to climb and intercept – one Squadron is waiting N.W. of Ile de Batz very high to intercept on return". It was then too late to recall the a/c.

At this point both aircraft could see a large patch of cloud in front. MUD 466 swerving to the right so as to leave the cloud on its port side and heading for the NORTH of USHANT and MUD 857 swerving to the left heading for the SOUTH OF USHANT. Both aircraft swung round to the left so as to approach BREST from the WEST, but, the cloud having been interposed between them neither saw the other again.

P/O Mulligan was dissatisfied with the distant approach to the target and MUD 857 made several fairly abrupt changes of course in an attempt to get a good bombing run. He finally succeeded in doing this and was satisfied that his aim was good and that the bombs would fall very near to the target. Neither of the three members of the crew so far interrogated (P/O STURMEY, P/O FRANKS, AND P/O MULLIGAN) saw the bombs fall, but F/SGT. GOLDSMITH (who is still in hospital) told them that he saw one burst on the Quay close to the ships (the exact position cannot be pin-pointed. The bombs were dropped at 1106 hours from 32,000 ft. on a course of 080° true. The fourth bomb momentarily "held up" but should not have overshot by any great distance.

Just before the bombs were dropped flak was observed about 3,000 feet above the aircraft and in front of it. When the aircraft was over the target and turning away to the left further flak was observed, this time very accurate for height but slightly to starboard.

THE COMBAT.

At 1109 two aircraft which F/ST. GOLDSMITH later identified as HE.113's were sighted. These emerged through light cloud about 1,000 feet below the Fortress and slightly to starboard. They were soon joined by five ME.109 F's; all seven aircraft appearing to come from the same general direction. A series of wide quarter attacks were made from one side or the other, with further attacks from dead astern. No accurate account of the combat can be given, partly because events were too confused and partly because the three members of the crew who have so far been interrogated saw little of what was happening behind.

It is understood that F/SGT. GOLDSMITH (who is a very reliable man) is satisfied that two of the five enemy aircraft were HE.113's.

The Fortress's upper backward firing guns still failed to fire (reason not known).

At about 1114 hours SGT. AMBROSE was hit in the thigh and perhaps elsewhere as well, and soon afterwards SGTS. NEEDLE and LEAHY were hit, and the later, (it is thought) in the head or neck, and the former in the stomach. SGT. AMBROSE probably died at once, but SGT. NEEDLE continued to send S.O.S. messages. He also put the I.F.F. on "broad band".

Meanwhile P/O STURMEY was taking all the avoiding action he could by swinging rapidly from side to side and varying his rate of descent. Realising that his only course was to get to sea level, he lost height as quickly as he could (about 2,000 feet per minute). His general course varied between about 320° and 040°.

The Fortress was followed down by the enemy aircraft which were repeatedly hitting it. No.4 petrol tank was punctured and the crew thought the engine had caught fire. Indeed there seemed to be no part of the aircraft which was not hit.

All attacks that were made were made either from a wide quarter (on either side) or from dead astern. Once however, one E/A passed in front of and below the Fortress and P/O MULLIGAN took advantage of the occasion to fire at it with the two side front guns. The mid-forward gun still failed to function. At about 30 miles SOUTH OF STARTPOINT however at 1130 hours approximately the enemy aircraft broke off the combat, the Fortress being then at about 6,000 feet. Probably the enemy thought the Fortress was plunging straight for the sea, as black smoke was pouring from it when it entered a thin patch of cloud that fortunately presented itself.

As far as is known none of the enemy aircraft was seriously damaged and perhaps none of them was hit.

THE FLIGHT HOME AND THE LANDING.

As soon as the combat had been broken off F/SGT. GOLDSMITH (who had been wounded by shrapnel in the left hand and left leg) attempted to go aft to see to the other members of the crew. This was an extremely hazardous task, as the guide ropes alongside the gangway had been shot away and the gangway itself was covered with a tangled mass of wires and cables. F/SGT. GOLDSMITH had to be restrained, almost by force, from making the attempt.

P/O MULLIGAN then tried to cross the gangway, but as a slip seemed almost inevitable he went back (when half-way over) for his parachute. Later he made a second attempt, but this time his parachute became entangled.

On reaching the English coast P/O STURMEY (who still thought No.4 engine might be slight) made for the nearest aerodrome. ROBOROUGH was smaller than he hoped it would be, and his difficulties were greatly increased because his flaps were U/S his tail tabs had been shot away, his bomb doors were side open, his tail wheel was stuck half up and half down and his brakes would not work. Only one aileron was serviceable. Further he had great difficulty in controlling his rudder. With much valuable help from P/O FRANKS however he succeeded in getting down.

In its final run the aircraft hit a hedge and a tank trap (which it carried away with it, a concrete slab being thrown on to a policeman) and on coming to rest it burst into flames.

AFTER THE CRASH.

P/O's STURMEY, FRANKS and MULLIGAN were soon out but all three climbed back into the after part of the burning plane to pull out the other members of the crew. F/SGT. GOLDSMITH who had also got out quickly, also tried to do the same. They also received much valuable help from a Lt. J.M. Allison of the 70th OXFORD & BUCKS. DEMFORD CAMP, CROWNHILL, SGT. LEAHY was still alive (although he died later in hospital). The other two were dead.

The Fortress is largely burnt out but parts of it (including the I.F.F. set complete with detonators) are left.

(Signed)   R.J.F. Burrows
(F/Lt.)

Polebrook.   18th Aug. 1941.

The following report on the operations of AN525 on 16 August has been reproduced verbatim:

F/Sgt. Goldsmith's Statement of the Attack by Fighters over BREST on FORTRESS I of 90 SQUADRON, POLEBROOK. On the 16th August, 1941 (N.S.I. MUD 8577 Note:- F/Sgt. Goldsmith was fire-controller in Fortress.

Sighted enemy fighters at 32,000 feet.

"Ack, Ack" dropped away directly below (very accurate and intense.)

Two aircraft approaching Port Quarter 5,000 ft. below. These fighters were very fast on the climb.

Order guns to "Stand by."

Enemy aircraft reached Fortress height and attacked in

formation "Dead astern" closed to 300 yards, Fire Controller hit in first attack.

Identified fighter as HE.113A, camouflage – all black excepting for tail fin which was painted yellow.

Four attacks were made from "Astern", average closing range 300 yards, all attacks made in formation. Vapour trails were continuous throughout both fighters and bombers.

Sgt. Leahy hit in the third attack, Sgt. Ambrose unable to fire owing to vapour trails (beam gunner). Sgt. Leahy did not say that he was hit, but his microphone was switched on and the "Fire Controller" could hear him groaning.

During the combat the Ack Ack ceased completely.

The enemy aircraft attacked again, broke away beneath and climbed up to attack from Astern and slightly below.

Evasive action was carried out from the Port to Starboard by turning, height was maintained throughout the engagement.

The Fortress was hit several times in this attack with cannon and machine gun. Combat lasted 7 minutes.

He.113A broke away and two 109F's attacked immediately from Starboard Quarter.

Sgt. Ambrose was hit seven or eight times in this attack. Sgt. Needle was unable to get his guns to work (freezing suspected). Sgt. Needle immediately on request from the Fire Controller sent an S.O.S. which was received in this country.

109Fs closed to 150 yards firing from Starboard and Port quarters, Sgt. Needle again manned mid-upper guns but was hit by a cannon shell. The 109Fs broke away and two more 109F's attacked, height still being maintained 32,000 feet. Evasive action taken by turning. Hits were obtained in the wing and fuselage. The 109Fs then delivered attacks from above on the wide quarters, Astral Dome hit by a cannon shell.

Attack broke off at 32,000 feet, duration of combat 12 minutes, camouflage of 109Fs – all black, excepting nose and tail fin which was yellow.

Last attack delivered immediately the previous two 109Fs broke off by one 109F. In this attack Fortress made for sea level in a straight dive.

The camouflage of this 109F was as follows:- Yellow nose and tail fin. Black fuselage with a red crest on each side.

ME.109F attacking from Quarter Astern to 8,000 ft. closing to 100 yards. Hits were obtained on Fortress. Attack broke off and Fortress levelled out at approximately 2,500 ft.

Total time of combat – 23 minutes.

GENERAL.

After the combats broke off the Fire Controller looked aft and noticed Sgt. Needle in a kneeling position with his hands clasped to his stomach.

Sgt. Leahy was still groaning and Fire Controller attempted to render first aid, but was unable to do so as the bomb compartment was opened and the rope rail was missing. The Fire Controllers leg was useless.

Observer tried to get through, but was unable to do so. During this period and previous period petrol was pouring out of the Starboard inner tanks.

Vapour trails started at 25,000 feet and continued until Fortress dived for the sea level.

Enemy aircraft had vapour trails. Engines were running well throughout engagements, until reaching the English coast when aircraft became unstable, rudder was smashed and wings and fuselage peppered with cannon and machine gun.

The HE.113s seemed to have a greater rate of climbing than the 109Fs.

109Fs favoured attacking from Starboard Quarter, this may have been due to the fact that in taking the correct avoiding action the Fortress would be heading back towards the enemy coast. The Fire Controller counteracted this by turning and straightening out immediately, thus heading in the general direction of the English coast.

Astral Dome frozen. Oxygen O.K.

Temperatures not too extreme.

Note:- This statement obtained by F/Lt. Meyer, Gunnery Leader of 90 Squadron, 21st August, 1941.

The following report from H.Q. Bomber Command on the Fortress I attack on the *Scharnhorst* and *Gneisenau* on 16 August 1941 has been reproduced verbatim:

> Serial No. ...... A.91-96.
> Page 3
> Date .... 17th September, 1941.

H.Q. Bomber Command.
    Royal Air Force.

COMMAND ROUTINE ORDERS

By

AIR MARSHALL SIR RICHARD E.C. PEIRSE, K.C.B., D.S.O., A.F.C.

A.94.   Notable War Services.

The Commander-in-Chief desires to bring to notice of all ranks in the Command the commendable courage and devotion to duty displayed by the crew of Fortress I aircraft, AN 523.

The aircraft was returning from a daylight attack on the battle cruisers GNEISENAU and SCHARNHORST at Brest on the morning of 16th August, 1941, when it was attacked by two Hes.113, which were joined a few minutes later by five Me.109Fs. Between them these seven enemy aircraft made 26 separate attacks on the Fortress at heights varying from 32,000 feet down to 8,000 ft., and lasting in all for 23 minutes.

During the latter attacks there was no return fire from the Fortress, as the Under-Gunner and Beam-Gunner were killed or mortally wounded in the earlier attacks, and the upper guns had become unserviceable. During the action, almost every part of the Fortress was hit by cannon shells or machine-gun bullets, and the outer starboard engine was thought to have caught fire.

The Wireless Operator/Upper Gunner manned the twin upper guns until they jammed. He then returned to his instrument and transmitted S.O.S. messages until he himself was killed. The Fire Controller, although himself wounded, continued from the astrodome to direct the avoiding action, and it was due to him that the Fortress was still flying and the first and second Pilot and Navigator were still unhurt when the engagement was broken off 30 miles from the English Coast.

The Fire Controller and Navigator then made plucky but unsuccessful attempts to reach the dead or dying members of the crew by crossing the gangway leading to the afterpart of the aircraft. This was a task involving extreme danger, as the gangway had become tangled with wrecked wires and cables and the guide ropes had been shot away; with the bomb-bay doors open there was nothing between this gangway and the sea below.

In view of the damage sustained by the aircraft it was decided to land at the first available aerodrome. Unfortunately, this proved to be a small one, with a rough surface and without runways while the damage sustained had rendered the Fortress difficult to control. The flaps were unserviceable, a piece of fabric 4 feet square had been ripped from the rudder, one aileron control had been shot away, the bomb-doors were open, the tail wheel had stuck in a half-retracted position, and the brakes would not work. In addition, a shell burst in the top of the cockpit had broken the radio compass mounted on the cockpit ceiling, the fluid thus released spraying the instrument panel so as to make a number of instruments unreadable.

In spite of this, the first and second Pilots succeeded in touching down safely. The aircraft overshot, however, and, hitting a steel and concrete tank-trap which had been concealed from view on the far side of the aerodrome, burst into flames. The two pilots, Navigator and Fire Controller re-entered the burning aircraft and with the help of an Army Officer who arrived on the scene, succeeded in removing the casualties. One of the latter, the Under-Gunner, was still alive when removed but died some hours later in hospital.

The crew consisted of:

Pilot Officer F.W. STURMEY	-	Captain
Pilot Officer T. FRANKS	-	2nd Pilot
Pilot Officer A.J. MULLIGAN (89770)	-	Navigator
527384 F/Sgt. N.F.T. GOLDSMITH	-	Fire Controller
983086 Sgt. H. NEEDLE	-	W.Op./Under Gunner
647891 Sgt. M.J. LEAHY	-	Under Gunner
646435 Sgt. S. AMBROSE	-	Beam Gunner

(Sgd.)

Air Vice Marshall,
1 o Administration
Bomber Command.

The German Battlecruisers *Scharnhorst* (above) and *Gneisenau*, lying in Brest Harbour, were a constant thorn in the side of the Admiralty; much of Bomber Commands effort being directed towards their destruction or damage. USN

At 15.30 hours that same day, 16 August, two Fortress I's, AN529 (C) (Sgt. Wood, Sgt. Hindshaw, Sgt. Sutton, Sgt. Danby, Sgt. Imrie, Sgt. Timlin and Sgt. Clifford) and AN536 (M) (P/O Taylor, P/O Hart, Sgt. Corbett, Sgt. Brown, Sgt. Honey, Sgt. Williams and Sgt. Merrille), took off for a high altitude attack on Dusseldorf. En-route to the target adverse weather conditions were encountered, "bad icing with cloud tops above 26,000 ft." The guns of AN529 froze and one of the gunner's heated clothing suit failed. It was decided to abort the mission and both aircraft turned for home with their bombs - 4 x 1,100 lb. each; AN536 landing at 16.45 followed by AN529 at 17.00 hours.

Top: A Fortress I from 90 Squadron takes off from Polebrook to attack the *Gneisenau* at Brest. Above: Long after the Fortress I was withdrawn from bombing operations over Europe Bomber Command heavies continued to attack the German Battlecruisers in Brest. Halifax's are here bombing the warships on 18 December 1941. RAF

There were no further operations until the 19th when two Fortress I's, AN529 (C) (Sgt. Wood, Sgt. Hindshaw, Sgt. Sutton, Sgt. Danby, Sgt. Imrie, F/Sgt. Timlin and Sgt. Clifford) and AN532 (J) (P/O Wayman, P/O McDonald, P/O Cotton, Sgt. Peggs, Sgt. Weil, Sgt. Street and Sgt. Jones), took off between 05.42 and 05.44 hours, with the intention of conducting a high altitude attack on Dusseldorf.

When in position 51° 52'N 03° 18'E AN529 (C) aborted the mission due to most of the aircraft's guns freezing and vapor trails forming when between 25,000 and 35,000 ft. The aircraft returned to base with its load of 4 x 1,100 lb. bombs, landing at 08.09 hours. AN532 (J) aborted when in position 51° 55'N 03° 18'E due to vapour trials forming between 25,000 and 35,000 ft. and 10/10ths low cloud cover over the Dutch coast. This aircraft returned to base with its 4 x 1,100 lb. bombs, landing at 08.45 hours.

The high altitude attacks on targets in Dusseldorf were attempted again on 21 August with three Fortress I's, AN536 (M) (S/Ldr. Mathieson, Sgt. Sleath, P/O Nesbit, Sgt. Willis, Sgt. James, Sgt. Allan and Sgt. Davis), AN532 (J) (P/O Wayman, P/O McDonald, P/O Cotton, Sgt. Peggs, Sgt. Weil, Sgt. Street and Sgt. Jones) and AN518 (B) (Sgt. Wood, Sgt. Hindshaw, Sgt. Sutton, Sgt. Clifford, Sgt. Imrie, Sgt. Danby and Sgt. Timlin). AN518 took off at 06.45 followed by AN536 at 06.50 then AN532 at 06.55 hours.

When in the Flushing area at an altitude of 35,000 ft. 9/10ths to 10/10ths cloud was noted beneath AN536 (M) and condensation trails were constantly forming between 26,000 ft. and 35,000 ft., and several guns had frozen, therefore, the mission was aborted and the aircraft returned to base with 4 x 1,100 lb. bombs, landing at 10.10 hours.

The turbo superchargers on both the port and starboard inboard engines of AN532 failed when the aircraft was in the area around Dordrecht at 36,000 ft. The mission was aborted and the aircraft returned to base, ditching its 4 x 1,100 lb. bombs in the North Sea before landing at 10.15 hours.

When in position 52° 05'N 02° 51'E at an altitude of 30,000 ft. AN518 aborted the mission due to vapour trails persistently forming and most of the guns freezing. The aircraft returned to base with its 4 x 1,100 lb. bombs, landing at 09.20 hours.

Yet another high altitude bombing attack against targets in Dusseldorf was attempted on 29 August. Two Fortress I's, AN533 (Sgt. Wood, Sgt. Hindshaw, Sgt. Sutton, Sgt. Clifford, Sgt. Imrie, Sgt. Danby and Sgt. Timlin) and AN536 (M) (P/O Wayman, P/O McDonald, P/O Cotton, Sgt. Peggs, Sgt. Weil, Sgt. Street and Sgt. Jones), were each armed with 4 x 1,100 lb. demolition bombs. This attempt would fare no better than the previous ones. AN533 unsuccessfully attempted to take off at 06.20 hours, but the aircraft failed to get airborne "owing to running away of turbo supercharger on No. 1 Engine, causing excessive swing". The second aircraft, AN536 (M), got airborne at 06.20 hours and proceeded towards the target, but aborted when in position 51° 50'N

04° 00'E at an altitude of 33,000 ft. due to condensation trails forming and 10/10ths cloud and a loss of manifold pressure on the No.2 and No.3 engines. The aircraft returned to base with its 4 x 1,100 lb. bombs, landing at 09.37 hours

The run of bad luck of the previous weeks continued when the last missions of the month were flown on 31 August with only marginal success being claimed. Three Fortress I's were flown against three separate targets. AN525 (D) (S/Ldr. Mathieson, Sgt. Sleath, P/O Nisbit, Sgt. Davis, Sgt. James, Sgt. Willis and Sgt. Allan) took off at 14.54 hours to conduct a high altitude attack on targets in Hamburg. En-route to the target the aircraft suffered oil trouble in the No.1 engine at 30,000 ft. Aborting the primary target, "a square search was made in the vicinity of Heligoland", and the aircraft dropped its 4 x 1,100 lb. bombs on Spiekeroog Island, from an altitude of 30,000 ft., all being noted to land in the sea. The aircraft then returned to base, landing at 19.58 hours.

AN518 (B) (Sgt. Wood, Sgt. Hindshaw, Sgt. Sutton, Sgt. Danby, Sgt. Imrie, Sgt. Clifford and F/Sgt. Timlin) took off at 14.53 hours for a high altitude attack on targets in Bremen. The target was reached and the 4 x 1,100 lb. bombs were dropped from an altitude of 31,000 ft., the bombs hanging up momentarily before jettisoning. The results of the bombing was unobserved due to cloud obscuring the target. The Fortress encountered no anti-aircraft fire or attacks by fighters and returned to base, landing at 20.09 hours.

AN532 (J) (F/O Wayman, P/O McDonald, P/O Cotton, Sgt. Peggs, Sgt. Weil, Sgt. Street and Sgt. Jones) took off at 14.51 hours for a high altitude attack on targets in Kiel, Germany, but when at 32,000 ft. the aircraft suffered turbo problems with No's 1, 3 and 4 engines and abandoned the primary target. When in the vicinity of Heligoland the aircraft was subjected to "heavy" flak and the aircraft continued to Den Helder, North Holland, but cloud prevented bombing. The aircraft then returned to base with its 4 x 1,100 lb. bombs, landing at 19.51 hours.

On all three mission no vapour trails, which had plagued previous missions, were noted to form. This may have indicated that afternoon operations were more suited to the high altitude missions being conducted, at least at the time of year and climatic conditions which prevailed during the last few weeks of August 1941.

On 2 September, three Fortress I's were tasked to attack three separate targets. AN518 (B) (Sgt. Wood, Sgt. Hindshaw, Sgt. Sutton, Sgt. Johnston, Sgt. Timlin, Sgt. Clifford and Sgt. Wilkins) took off at 13.30 hours for a high altitude attack on targets in Duisburg, Germany. When in the area of Newbury the aircraft aborted due to an intercom failure, landing back at base at 15.00 hours.

AN533 (N) (S/Ldr. Mathieson, Sgt. Sleath, P/O Nisbet, Sgt. Davis, Sgt. James, Sgt. Willis, Sgt. Allan and a Mr. Vose (from the Sperry Bombsight Co. in the United States who was acting as bomb aimer) took off at 14.00 hours for a high altitude attack against targets in Bremen. On reaching the target area the

Fortress dropped its load of 4 x 1,100 lb. bombs from an altitude of 30,000 ft. One of the bombs landed in the town of Bremen, but the other three were noted to land outside the town. When leaving the target area the aircraft was subjected to heavy flak which continued until the aircraft reached the German coast. The aircraft returned to base and landed at 19.00 hours.

AN532 (J) (P/O Sturmey, P/O Franks, P/O Mulligan, F/Sgt. Mennie, Sgt. Hugill, Sgt. Pawsey and Sgt. Birtwhistle) took off at 14.05 hours, and, when passing between 25,000 and 30,000 ft. the aircraft encountered 10/10ths cloud then noted vapour trails forming resulting in the operation being aborted, the aircraft returning to base with its 4 x 1,100 lb. bombs, landing at 17.10 hours.

The next missions took place on 4 September when two Fortress's were tasked with high altitude attacks on targets in Hanover and a single Fortress was tasked to conduct a high altitude attack on Hamburg.

AN533 (N) (P/O Romans, P/O Hart, Sgt. Corbett, Sgt. Honey, Sgt. Brown, Sgt. Merrill and Sgt. Williams) and AN532 (J) (P/O Sturmey, P/O Franks, P/O Mulligan, F/Sgt. Mennie, Sgt. Hugill, Sgt. Pawsey and Sgt. Britwhistle) took off from Polebrook at 14.20 and 14.10 hours respectively to attack Hanover. When at 31,000 ft. AN533 aborted the primary target due to vapour trails forming, the aircraft's 4 x 1,100 lb. bombs being dropped on the docks at Rotterdam, Holland. The aircraft encountered flak and noted a pair of German Me.109 fighters, which were lost when the Fortress entered a 1,500 feet per minute climb. The aircraft returned to base and landed at 17.35 hours.

AN532 (J) suffered a failure of the No.1 engine at 30,000 ft. when around 60 miles from Heligoland, the mission then being aborted, the 4 x 1,100 lb. bombs being ditched in the sea, after which the bomb bay doors would not close, being eventually wound shut by hand. En-route to base the engine "picked up" when at an altitude of 20,000 ft. The aircraft landed back at base at 17.30 hours.

AN518 (B) (Sgt. Wood, Sgt. Hindshaw, Sgt. Sutton, Sgt. Johnston, Sgt. Timlin, Sgt. Clifford and Sgt. Wilkins) took off at 14.10 hours and headed for Hamburg, but aborted the mission when at 15,000 ft., some 50 miles from the Norfolk coast due to an intercom failure. The aircraft returned to Polebrook and landed at 15.40 hours.

As plans were developed for an high altitude of attack on the German Pocket Battleship (11-in gun heavy Cruiser) *Admiral Sheer* lying in harbor in Oslo, Norway, elements of No.90 Squadron along with five Fortress I's moved north to RAF Kinloss, Morayshire, in the north of Scotland in preparation for the mission. The Fortress I's consisted of AN525, AN532, AN533, AN536 and AN535, the latter carrying ground crew.

The attack against the *Admiral Sheer* commenced when four Fortress I's, AN533 (N) (S/Ldr. Mathieson, Sgt. Sleath, P/O Hogan, Sgt. Davies, Sgt. James, Sgt. Willis and Sgt. Allan), AN525 (D) (P/O Romans, F/O Hart, Sgt. Corbett, Sgt. Honey, Sgt. Brown, Sgt. Merrill and Sgt. Williams), AN532 (J) (P/O

Sturmey, P/O Franks, P/O Mulligan, F/Sgt. Mennie, Sgt. Hugill, Sgt. Pawsey and Sgt. Birtwhistle) and AN536 (M) (Sgt. Wood, Sgt. Hindshaw, Sgt. Sutton, Sgt. Johnston, Sgt. Timlin, Sgt. Clifford and Sgt. Wilkins) took off from Kinloss at 08.00 hours on the morning of 6 September.

AN536 (M) suffered problems with the turbo on No.3 engine and aborted the mission when at 15,000 ft. and 50 miles out from base. The aircraft returned to Kinloss with its 4 x 1,100 lb. bombs, landing at 09.30 hours.

AN533 (N) failed to locate the target, dropping its load of 4 x 1,100-lb. bombs on the Oslo docks and oil tanks from 30,000 ft. then returning to Kinloss, where it landed at 13.45 hours.

AN525 (D) also failed to locate the target, and, like AN533, dropped its 4 x 1,100 lb. bombs on the docks at Oslo before returning to Kinloss where it landed at 13.20, suffering a failure of the No.2 engine just before it landed.

As with the other two aircraft, AN532 (J) failed to locate the target and dropped its four x 1,100 lb. bombs on Oslo docks before returning to Kinloss where it landed at 13.25 hours.

None of the Fortress's encountered ground fire or enemy fighters. Vapour trails were noted to have formed above 30,000 ft.

The same mission was scheduled again for the 8th; the same aircraft and crews with the exception that Sgt. Beatty replaced Sgt. Williams in AN525 (D) and the crew of AN536, captained by Sgt. Wood on the 6th, now flew in AN535.

Three of the Fortress's, AN525, AN532 and AN535, took off from Kinloss at 09.15 hours followed ten minutes later by AN533 (N). This last mentioned aircraft was never seen again after it took off and no messages were received indicating any mechanical problems.

AN525 (D) was noted to be under attack by a pair of Luftwaffe Me.109's while at 25,000 ft. over Norway at 11.27 hours. The German fighters shot the Fortress down, the latter being observed "to crash in flames". It was initially claimed that one of the Me.109's crashed along with the Fortress, however, this was probably just following the stricken bomber down.

AN532 (J) reached a point about 80 miles from Oslo before aborting the mission at an altitude of 27,500 ft. due to encountering 10/10ths cloud cover. It was the crew of this aircraft which had observed the German fighters shoot down AN525 (D). AN532 returned to Kinloss with its 4 x 1,100 lb. bombs, landing at 13.35 hours.

AN535 had no better luck, aborting the mission at 11.30 hours, the aircraft jettisoning its bombs over Norwegian mountains before climbing to 34,000 ft. in order to evade German fighters trying to intercept. Unfortunately a failure of the oxygen system compelled the pilot to descend to 24,000 ft. where the Fortress was attacked by a single Me.109 fighter which pressed its attack to close range inflicting a number of hits on the Fortress. One of the crew, Sgt. Wilkin, was killed and another, F/Sgt. Tait, injured in the attack. On the homeward flight the No.1 and No.3 engines failed and the aircraft limped back to crash land at Kinloss.

The operations against the *Admiral Sheer* had proved to be a total failure. None of the aircraft had reached the target, two Fortress's had been lost and a third seriously damaged for no return. Furthermore, intelligence reports showed the Sheer to have left Oslo on 7 September, one day before the disastrous operation of the 8th.

The Luftwaffe claimed two Fortress's shot down, 1 each by 13./JG-77 and 2./JG-77 about 75 and 50 miles from Stavanger, Norway, respectively. One of these aircraft was AN525 (D), the other was probably AN535 which was attacked and damaged by a German fighter, but managed to limp home to Kinloss where it crash landed.

Following these losses, combined with the limited number of Fortress aircraft and trained crews on strength, the squadron was effectively non-operational for the next week as it licked its wounds. While a few more missions would be flown in the daylight high altitude bombing experiment, the writing was effectively on the wall for the Fortress I's career as a high altitude bomber with Bomber Command in the European Theatre.

The following report on Fortress I operations over Norway on 6 September 1941 has been reproduced verbatim:

REPORT 41/4477 (Handwritten)
OF OPERATIONS OF FORTRESS AIRCRAFT OVER NORWAY on 6th SEPTEMBER 1941.

---

1. Five aircraft, including one non-operational with maintenance crews, were ordered to fly to Kinloss on the afternoon of 5th September 1941 to attack the battleship Admiral Scheer which had been reported to be in Oslo Harbour.

2. Four aircraft of 90 Squadron (AN.533, S/Ldr. Mathieson; AN.525, F/O Romans; AN532, P/O Sturmey; AN.536, Sgt. Wood) were detailed to make the attack on the morning of 6th September 1941. They were to attack in company with a normal bomb load of four 1,100 lb. demolition bombs, fused instantaneous nose, 45 seconds delay tail. Instructions were given by headquarters, 2 Group, that condensation trails had to be ignored, but since they were estimated to be between 28,000 feet and 38,000 feet, the Squadron Commander gave instructions that the bombing was to be just below the condensation trail height if practicable. (A W/T signal was sent by Headquarters, 2 Group, addressed to S/Ldr. Mathieson's aircraft only as follows: "Suggest bomb at height for full automatic operation bomb sight," but this signal was

not received by him).

3.   The aircraft set course at 08.06 hours on 6th September 1941, but Sgt. Wood returned at 09.45 hours, one of his engines having lost power due to a fracture in the induction system. All three aircraft returned to Kinloss by 14.45 hours, having attacked between 10.10 hours and 10.50 hours from heights between 27,000 feet and 30,000 feet.

3.   None of the three aircraft identified its primary target: all attacked the last resort (illegible), instead.

4.   No anti-aircraft or fighter opposition was encountered except that several smoke trails, presumably enemy, were seen above the Fortresses over the target area.

5.   The routing of this attack was almost direct to the target and returning North-about, but two aircraft landed at Kinloss very short of petrol; one had one engine stopped taxying in and the other one had only five minutes more petrol, having flown at the most economical speed possible for the return journey.

The following report on Fortress I operations over Norway on 8 September 1941 has been reproduced verbatim:

REPORT
OF OPERATIONS OF FORTRESS AIRCRAFT OVER NORWAY ON 8TH SEPTEMBER, 1941.

1.   On the 8th September 1941 four aircraft of 90 Squadron (AN.533 S/Ldr. Mathieson; AN.525 F/O Romans; AN.532 P/O Sturmey; AN.535 Sgt. Wood) were again ordered to attack the Admiral Scheer in Oslo Harbour. It was suggested that the aircraft should attack from the maximum height (19,000 feet) for full operation of the automatic bomb sight, but, as they did not possess the R/2 Chart Sector the Squadron Commander decided to bomb instead at the lowest height (26,000 feet) for which the calculator at present in use can be used. The aircraft on this second attack were routed South-about, and were to return direct owing to the petrol shortage experienced after the first attack.

2.   Three aircraft (F/O Romans, P/O Sturmey and Sgt. Wood), set course at 09.20 hours and left in company; of these three only two, P/O Sturmey and Sgt. Wood, returned. S/Ldr. Mathieson set course

at 09.25 hours and therefore left alone; nothing further was heard of him.

3.   Approaching the Norwegian coast at 11.00 hours P/O. Sturmey and Sgt. Wood passed under an old condensation trail at 30,000 feet, running parallel to the coast. When the Norwegian coast was crossed at 11.03 hours, the three aircraft which left first had become slightly spread out; P/O Sturmey was leading at 27,000 feet, Sgt. Wood was two miles behind him at 22,000 feet and F/O Romans was a mile or two behind and seven miles to starboard at about 24,000 feet.

4.   Shortly afterwards P/O. Sturmey's intercom failed in three places.

5.   At 11.24 hours at 58 degs. 52 minutes North, 08 degs. 07 minutes East (120 miles South West of Oslo) P/O. Sturmey at 28,000 feet saw two SE fighters attacking F/O Romans who was now about five miles behind and slightly to port apparently at 24,000 feet. P/O. Sturmey observed F/O. Romans to return the enemy's fire and then to go down in a gradual dive without spinning, omitting a trail of black smoke. F/O. Romans was last seen when close to the ground and a considerable volume of smoke was afterwards seen on the ground at about that place, while another smaller smoke column with fire, was seen on the ground four miles away. No parachutes were seen.

6.   At 11.27 hours, about ten miles further East, P/O. Sturmey at 23,000 feet met a bank of cloud from 26,000 feet to 29,000 feet and turned back.

7.   At (illegible – assumed to be 59) degs. 12 minutes North 07 degs. 00 minutes East at 11.44 hours at 27,000 feet, P/O. Sturmey observed a large volume of grey smoke on the ground at a point five to ten miles south of the eastern end of Lyse Fjord.

8.   P/O. Sturmey landed at Kinloss at 13.24 hours, bringing his bombs back with him.

9.   Sgt. Wood confirms the relative positions of the three aircraft when crossing the Norwegian coast inward bound, as given in Paragraph 3. When about four miles behind P/O. Sturmey, at a point 2 miles south of Akernes (69 degs 45 mins north, 07 degs 30 mins east) at 1120 hours at 23,000 feet, Sgt. Wood saw two Me.109's attacking F/O. Romans about 2 or 3 miles behind him and to port and say 5,000 feet below him. F/O. Romans was not leaving vapour trails. F/O. Romans

was observed by Sgt. Wood to be turning hard to port with one enemy aircraft following 50 yards behind and the second enemy aircraft further behind. No further details of the encounter were observed by Sgt. Wood.

10.   Sgt. Wood then jettisoned his bombs safe (it is thought, however, that either 3 or 4 then exploded) and turned back. He had been making vapour trails almost continuously since crossing the Norwegian coast and now climbed to 35,000 feet to get rid of them. He recrossed the Norwegian coast at Eigeroe. At 58 degs 19 mins. North, 03 degs 52 mins. East (ie. 70 miles off the Norwegian coast at the nearest point) at 1200 hours at 35,000 feet the beam and mid-under gunners of his aircraft were found to be unconscious through lack of oxygen. Sgt. Wood put his nose down in a dive at an air speed of 288, losing height at 2,000 feet per minute. The vapour trail continued in the dive. When probably at 25,000 feet at 1205 hours, Sgt. Wood was approached from the stern by one Me.109E, which fired a long burst closing to 50 yards and then turned away to port and was not seen again. In this burst, Sgt. Wood's under gunner was killed and his beam gunner wounded and his aileron control and No.1 engine rendered u/s. Fire was not returned by Sgt. Wood.

11.   Sgt. Wood had considerable difficulty in regaining control of the aircraft but succeeded in doing so at 5.000 feet and returned to Kinloss at that height, with one airscrew fully feathered. He crash landed at Kinloss at 1403 hours, without further injury to his crew. The aircraft sustained further damage in the crash landing principally to under carriage and airscrews and to No.2 engine which was removed from its mounting.

12.   There is no question but that the interceptions described in paras 5 and 9 are one and the same in spite of differences of time and position. It is probable that the position reported by Sgt. Wood is the more accurate.

(Sgd)   ....
Group Captain, Commanding,
R.A.F. Station, Polebrook.

Pol/S.86/16/INT.

Following the losses of the 8th, No.90 Squadrons attempts to bomb the *Admiral Sheer* in Oslo harbor were abandoned, the Sheer having departed Oslo on the 7th, the remaining aircraft and personnel returning south where there was a resumption of high altitude bombing attacks against targets in north west Europe.

The first mission since the fateful events of the 8th was launched on 15 September when a single Fortress, AN536 (M) (P/O Wayman, P/O McDonald, P/O Cotton, Sgt. Peggs, Sgt. Weil, Sgt. Street and Sgt. Jones), took off on a high altitude attack against Cologne, Germany. When over the Dutch coast at 32,000 ft., the Fortress formed vapour trails resulting in the mission being aborted as vapour trails, assumed to be from German fighters, were noted heading in their direct. The aircraft returned to base with its 2 x 2,000 lb. bombs, landing at 16.00 hours.

On the 16th, AN536 (M) (P/O Sturmey, P/O Franks, P/O Mulligan, F/Sgt. Mennie, Sgt. Hugill, Sgt. Pawsey and Sgt. Birtwhistle), took off at 13.10 hours for a high altitude attack against Cologne, but the mission was aborted some thirty miles from the Dutch coast, attributed to "loss of power in No.2 engine, illness of Sgt. Birtwhistle, and observation of vapour trails of enemy fighters". The aircraft returned to base with its 2 x 2,000 lb. bombs, landing at 15.55 hours.

There were no more operations until the 20th, when Fortress I AN518 (B) with the same crew as the mission on the 16th, captained by P/O Sturmey, took off at 12.55 hours for a high altitude bombing attack against targets in Emden, Germany. The aircraft dropped its load of 4 x 1,100 lb. bombs from an altitude of 32,000 ft., smoke columns being observed to rise from the target area. Just prior to the bomb release, vapour trails from an unidentified aircraft were observed, but no ground fire was noted and no attacks by enemy fighters developed. The aircraft returned to base and landed at 17.15 hours.

Emden was again the target when AN518 (B), (P/O Sturmey, P/O Franks, P/O Mulligan, Sgt. Hugill, Sgt. Jones, F/Lt. Meyer and F/Lt. Bosdari - 2nd Navigator) took off at 12.00 hours on 25 September 1941. The mission, however, was aborted when some 50 miles from the Dutch coast at an altitude of 27,000 ft. due to vapour trails forming. During the return flight to base the electric suite of the ventral gunner caught fire, but the fire was extinguished, the aircraft then landing, with its 4 x 1,100 lb. bombs, at 15.00 hours.

This was the last operational mission flown over North West Europe by No.90 Squadron equipped with the Fortress I. An inauspicious end to the high altitude bombing campaign begun less than three months before. The Fortress I had proven to be unsuitable for operations at the altitudes it was designed to be flown at; inadequate armament which froze at the extreme cold which hampered many of the sorties and was set to worsen with the onset of winter. The Sperry bombsight was not accurate enough for operations at the high altitudes flown; No.90 Squadron had lost four aircraft either destroyed on operations or so extensity battle damaged that they were considered operational losses, with one other aircraft suffering battle damage for the poor return of a few bombs being placed in the general vicinity of the target areas.

Fortress AN532 at Shallufa, Egypt, in November 1941. A few months later this aircraft was transferred back to the USAAF. RAF

Hard lessons had been learned by both the RAF and the USAAF, the latter of which would fly mass daylight bombing raids with later, improved, models of the B-17 during the last few years of the war

In November 1941, a detachment of four No.90 Squadron Fortress I's were dispatched to Shallufa, Egypt, for night bombing operations against targets such as Benghazi, Cyrenaica, with a secondary anti-shipping role. The 90 Squadron detachment was re-designated No.220 Squadron Detachment on 1 December 1941.

4

POSTSCIRPT

The failure of the high altitude daylight bombing operations by the Fortress I equipped No.90 Squadron was not the end for the Fortress in RAF service. As noted previously a detachment of No.90 Squadrons surviving Fortress I's were sent to the Middle East, being transferred to No.220 Squadron Detachment, and others, following their retirement by No.90 Squadron, served with RAF Coastal command, 220 and 206 Squadrons, alongside later Fortress MK.II (B-17F) and Fortress MK.III's (B-17G), the latter model also serving Bomber Command with No.100 Bomber Support Group, the aircraft being fitted out as electronic warfare aircraft for jamming German radar.

The No.220 Squadron Detachment in the Middle East flew only a small number of operations, mainly against Italian convoys; one sortie claiming a near miss on an Italian Battleship with 500 lb. SAP bombs on 21 January 1942. The detachment had a few combats with German Me.110 twin-engine fighters, claiming one as probably destroyed (unconfirmed) on 22 February 1942.

In the daylight bomber role, the Fortress, in B-17E/F/G Flying Fortress guise, flew large scale bombing missions over Europe operating with the USAAF Eighth Air Force, typically from lower altitudes than those flown by the Fortress I, the first such missions being flown, with B-17E's, from Polebrook on 17 August 1942. The American operations were flown with better armed and better equipped aircraft which flew at lower altitude and for the most part with fighter escort, initially provided by RAF Fighter Command Spitfires before being joined by Eighth Fighter Command USAAF with longer range fighters like the Republic P-47 and North American P-51 Mustang.

Top: Some of the surviving Fortress I's were turned over to RAF Coastal Command. Here AN537of No.220 Squadron is flying a convoy protection patrol operating from Ballykelly, County Londonderry, Northern Ireland. The wartime censor has removed the radar aerials and unit code letters. RAF The small number of Fortress I's were soon dwarfed by deliveries of the more capable Fortress II (B-17F) and Fortress III (B-17G). Here Fortress III HB733 is at Prestwick, Ayrshire, Scotland. Although wearing RAF colours this aircraft never actually served with the RAF, being allocated to the USAAF Eighth Air Force operating in the daylight bomber role over Europe. MAP

APPENDICES

APPENDIX I

Fortress MK.I (Boeing B-17C) allocated to Britain

UK Serial	USAAC Serial
AN518 *	(40-2043)
AN519 *	(40-2044)
AN520	(40-2051)
AN521	(40-2052)
AN522 *	(40-2053)
AN523 *	(40-2055)
AN524	(40-2056)
AN525 *	(40-2057)
AN526 *	(40-2060)
AN527 *	(40-2061)
AN528 *	(40-2064)
AN529 *	(40-2065)
AN530 *	(40-2066)
AN531	(40-2068)
AN532 *	(40-2069)
AN533 *	(40-2071)
AN534 *	(40-2073)
AN535 *	(40-2075)
AN536 *	(40-2076)
AN537	(40-2079)

Serials with * are aircraft known to have served with No.90 Squadron between May and the end of September 1941.

APPENDIX II

Operational sorties flown by No.90 Squadron 8 July - 25 September 1941

	Sorties	Bombs dropped	Bombs jettisoned
July 1941	11	26	0
August 1941	23*	36	4
September 1941	18	24	8
Total	52	86	12

*Includes 1 planned sortie which failed to get airborne

APPENDIX III

No.90 Squadron Fortress I (B-17C) operational and non-operational losses from May to September 1941 (includes aircraft seriously damaged)

Aircraft	Date	Circumstances
AN522	22 June 1941	Pilot lost control in heavy weather and aircraft entered a dive and broke up
AN528	3 July 1941	Burnt out after engine caught fire during ground runs
AN534	28 July 1941	Crashed after taking off on an altitude climb test, all crew being killed
AN530	2 August 1941	Damaged after being attacked by 2 x Me.109F Fighters
AN523	16 August 1941	Attacked by enemy fighters and seriously damaged. Pilot made an emergency landing at Roborough, Plymouth, but the aircraft overshot on the landing and caught fire – three crew being killed and a fourth injured
AN533	8 September 1941	Aircraft took off from Kinloss to attack warship in Oslo harbor and was never seen again
AN532	8 September 1941	Aircraft was shot down by German Me.109 fighters while on the same mission as the above aircraft
AN535	8 September 1941	Suffered extensive damage after being attacked by a German Me.109 during an attempted high altitude bombing attack on the German Pocket Battleship (Heavy Cruiser) *Admiral Sheer* in Norway; crash landed at Kinloss, Scotland.

APPENDIC IV

Specification

Boeing B-17C (USAAF figures)

Engines: Four x Wright R-1820-65 turbo-supercharged radial engines each rated at 1,200 hp.
Span: 103 ft. 9 in
Length: 67 ft. 11 in
Height: 15 ft. 5 in
Weight: 48,500 lb. gross
Maximum speed: 287 mph at 23,000 ft. (figures vary in documents)
Cruise speed: 227 mph
Service ceiling 37,000 ft.
Range: 3,400 miles (figure is for ferry range)

Note: Fortress I's were, on a number of occasions, flown at altitudes up to 38,000 ft. (this altitude was reached without payload)

APPENDIX V

B-17C (USAAC figures)

Overall length: 67 ft. 10 9/19 in.
Overall height: 15 ft. 4 ½ in.
Overall span: 103 ft. 9 3/8 in.

Weight: normal design and maximum design			30,900 lb.	30,900 lb.
Crew and parachutes (6 at 200 lb.)			1,200 lb.	1,200 lb.

Engine: 4 x R-1820-65 nine-cylinder, geared radial air-cooled, supercharged engines

Engine ratings:

Takeoff	1200 BHP	2500 RPM	46"	Hg. MP
Sea Level	1000 BHP	2300 RPM	39.5"	Hg. MP
25,000 ft.	1000 BHP	2300 RPM	39.5"	Hg. MP

GLOSSARY

A/C	Aircraft
AG	Air Gunner
B	Bomber
CO	Commanding Officer
Degs.	Degrees
DFC	Distinguished Flying Cross
E	East
F/Lt.	Flight Lieutenant
F/O	Flying Officer
F/Sgt.	Flight Sergeant
He	Heinkel
HE	High Explosive
HH	His Highness
I	One
IFF	Identification Friend or Foe
II	Two
IV	Four
MAP	Ministry of Aircraft Production
Me	Messerschmitt
MO	Medical Officer
MU	Maintenance Unit
N	North
No.	Number
NW	North West
OTU	Operational Training Unit
P/O	Pilot Officer
RAF	Royal Air Force
SE	Single Engine
Sgt.	Sergeant
S/Ldr.	Squadron Leader
U/S	Unserviceable
USAAC	United States Army Air Corp
USAF	United States Air Force
USAAF	United States Army Air Force
USSR	Union of Soviet Socialist Republics
V	Five
VI	Six
W/Cdr.	Wing Commander
W/Op	Wireless Operator

BIBLIOGRAPHY

No.90 Squadron Operations Record Book Form 540 March 1937 – July 1941

No.90 Squadron Operations Record Book Form 540 August 1941

No.90 Squadron Operations Record Book Form 540 September 1941

No.90 Squadron Operations Record Book Form 541 July 1941

No.90 Squadron Operations Record Book Form 541 August 1941

No.90 Squadron Operations Record Book Form 541 September 1941

No.35 Squadron Operations Record Book Form 540 July 1941

No.90 Squadron Battle Order No.1, July 1941

No.90 Squadron Battle Order No.2, July 1941

Proceedings of Court of Inquiry into loss of Fortress I on 28 July 1941

Report on Operations by Fortress A.N.525 of 90 Squadron on Brest, 15th August, 1941

F/Sgt. Goldsmith's Statement of the Attack by Fighters over Brest on Fortress I of 90 Squadron, Polebrook on 16th August, 1941

Report 41/4477 of Operations of Fortress Aircraft over Norway on 6th September 1941

Report of Operations of Fortress Aircraft over Norway on 8th September, 1941

H.Q. Bomber Command, Routine Orders dated 17 September 1941

No.220 Squadron Detachment (Ex 90 Squadron Detachment) Operations Record Book Form 540 December 1941

No.220 Squadron Detachment (Ex 90 Squadron Detachment) Operations Record Book Form 540 1 January - 31 March 1941

History of the Second World War, The RAF 1939-45 Volume I, 1953 HMSO

W.P. (41) 160

W.P. (41) 166

W.P. (41) 179

W.P. (41) 184

W.P. (41) 189

W.P. (41) 194

W.P. (41) 199

W.P. (41) 207

W.P. (41) 214

W.P. (41) 218

W.P. (41) 223

W.P. (41) 226

W.P. (41) 231

In addition hundreds of miscellaneous pages of documents; development, operational, command and political were consulted.

ABOUT THE AUTHOR

Hugh, a historian and author, has published in excess of thirty books; non-fiction and fiction, writing under his own name as well as utilising two different pseudonyms. He has also written for several international magazines, whilst his work has been used as reference for many other projects ranging from the aviation industry, international news corporations, film media to encyclopedias and the computer gaming industry. He currently resides in his native Scotland

Other titles by the Author include

Hurricane IIB Combat Log - 151 Wing RAF, North Russia 1941
RAF Meteor Jet Fighters in World War II, an Operational Log
Typhoon IA/B Combat Log - Operation Jubilee, August 1942
Defiant MK.I Combat Log - Fighter Command, May-September 1940
Blenheim MK.IF Combat Log - Fighter Command Day Fighter Sweeps/Night Interceptions - September 1939 - June 194
Tomahawk I/II Combat Log - European Theatre - 1941-42
Eurofighter Typhoon - Storm over Europe
Sukhoi Su-34 'Fullback' - Russia's 21st Century Striker
Tornado F.2/F.3 Air Defence Variant
British Battlecruisers of World War 1 - Operational Log, July 1914-June 1915
Boeing X-36 Tailless Agility Flight Research Aircraft
X-32 - The Boeing Joint Strike Fighter
X-35 - Progenitor to the F-35 Lightning II
X-45 Uninhabited Combat Air Vehicle
North American F-108 Rapier
F-84 Thunderjet - Republic Thunder
USAF Jet Powered Fighters - XP-59-XF-85
XF-92 - Convairs Arrow
The Battle Cruiser Fleet at Jutland
Light Battlecruisers and the 2nd Battle of Heligoland Bight
Saab Gripen, The Nordic Myth
American Teens
Dassault Rafale, The Gallic Squall
Boeing F/A-18E/F Super Hornet